HISTORIC GREGG COUNTY

An Illustrated History

By Van Craddock, Jr.

—To Molly and David
Hope you enjoy the book!
Van Craddock
2006

Commissioned by the Gregg County Historical Commission

Historical Publishing Network
A division of Lammert Incorporated
San Antonio, Texas

Downtown Gladewater during the oil-boom days was typical of the frenzied activity of the era. The town's population increased from five hundred to several thousand with discovery of oil.

COURTESY OF THE GREGG COUNTY HISTORICAL MUSEUM.

First Edition

ISBN: 9781893619623

Library of Congress Card Catalog Number: 2006931086

Historic Gregg County: An Illustrated History

author: Van Craddock, Jr.

contributing writers for "Sharing the Heritage": Eric Dabney, Scott Williams

Historical Publishing Network

president: Ron Lammert

project manager: Wynn Buck

director of operations: Charles A. Newton III

administration: Donna M. Mata, Diane Perez

book sales: Dee Steidle

graphic production: Colin Hart, Charles A. Newton III, Craig Mitchell, Michael Reaves, John Barr, Evelyn Hart

PRINTED IN SINGAPORE.

Dedication

At the time this book was going to press, Dr. Norman W. Black, chairman of the Gregg County Historical Commission and longtime county resident, became ill and ultimately passed away on December 11, 2005. Dr. Black, a local Longview dentist, noted historian, and good friend to so many, will be sorely missed. It is with humility that we, on behalf of Gregg County, dedicate this book, of which he worked so diligently in its publication, in Dr. Black's loving memory.

Bill Stoudt
Gregg County Judge

Contents

This red-brick courthouse was opened in 1897 and served residents until 1932, when the oil boom necessitated a larger structure. Note that the Confederate monument had been relocated from Bodie Park to its present location on the courthouse lawn.

COURTESY OF THE GREGG COUNTY HISTORICAL MUSEUM.

Acknowledgments

Thank you to Gregg County Judge Bill Stoudt and the commissioners court, as well as Chairman Dr. W. D. Northcutt III and the Gregg County Historical Commission, for their support of this endeavor. Thanks also to the Gregg County Historical Museum, East Texas Oil Museum at Kilgore College, *Longview News-Journal*, *Kilgore News Herald*, *Gladewater Mirror*, Longview Public Library, Kilgore Public Library and Gladewater's Lee Library for their help.

Please let me single out the historical museum's Glenda Wood, Ann Rast and Dave Bennett for their invaluable help with photos and, of course, those businesses and individuals who have supported this book through their participation.

This book is not intended as a comprehensive history but does touch on many of the people, places and events that have made Gregg County history so compelling. For further reading on the subject, I highly recommend Eugene W. McWhorter's *Traditions of the Land: The History of Gregg County* (1989) published by the Gregg County Historical Foundation.

This book is respectfully dedicated to the late Dr. Norman Black, longtime chair of the Gregg County Historical Commission, whose tireless efforts ensured the preservation of so much local history. He even designed Gregg County's official flag, adopted in 1988. Dr. Black is missed.

Van Craddock, Jr.

This 1909 photo shows the interior of Longview's "uptown" Texas & Pacific depot. Seated is L.L. Eddings; standing is ticket agent J.H. Hurst.

COURTESY OF THE GREGG COUNTY HISTORICAL MUSEUM.

Considered the first organized church in what became Gregg County, Pine Tree Cumberland Presbyterian Church traces its roots back to 1847. The first pastor was Reverend Solomon Awalt. This frame building served the congregation from 1858 until the 1930s.

COURTESY OF THE GREGG COUNTY HISTORICAL MUSEUM.

Chapter I

In the Beginning — A 'No Man's Land'

In less than a century, Gregg County went from a sparsely inhabited wilderness to America's largest oil-producing county. It is a remarkable story. Gregg County was officially organized in April 1873, but development of this pine-studded East Texas area began centuries earlier.

After the Louisiana Purchase of 1803, the United States and Spain couldn't agree on the boundary between Texas and Louisiana. East Texas was a true "no-man's land." Three years later, a treaty officially declared the area to be "neutral ground" with neither nation having jurisdiction. What is now Gregg County lay on the northern end of the neutral ground, which quickly became a haven for large numbers of smugglers and bandits many miles from legal authorities. By 1810 the two governments had to send in troops to quell the ne'er-do-wells. However, the neutral ground continued to be lawless long after ownership of the area was awarded to the U.S. in 1821.

Native Americans, notably the Caddoes and Cherokees, had lived in the area for many years before Anglo settlers began to arrive in the 1820s and 1830s. The Caddoes, in fact, had settled in the Pineywoods hundreds of years before the Spanish or French ever sniffed around this part of the world. A peaceful people, the Caddoes loved the East Texas forests, living in permanent, spacious huts that sometimes were fifty feet in diameter. They were adept hunters with bow and arrow. They were agrarian, growing corn and beans, and made beautiful pottery. Unlike many tribes, women often held positions of influence in Caddoan tribal affairs. Other tribes knew the Caddoes as the "Pierced Nose" for their habit of wearing metal rings in the nose and ears. When visitors came into their villages, they were fed, entertained and given gifts.

The Cherokees had been uprooted from their homes in the Southeastern United States and forced West in 1820. For many, East Texas became the promised land. The area had plenty of rivers and lots of

❖

Caddo houses were permanent, spacious huts that sometimes spanned 50 feet in diameter. The Caddoes were known by other tribes as the "Pierced Nose" for their habit of wearing metal rings.

COURTESY OF THE GREGG COUNTY HISTORICAL MUSEUM.

❖

Above: The Caddoes were an agrarian, peaceful people who lived in East Texas hundreds of years before the Spanish or French arrived in the area. "Caddo" is a contraction of their tribal name of Kadohadacho, which settlers found too difficult to pronounce.

COURTESY OF THE GREGG COUNTY HISTORICAL MUSEUM.

Below: The stately colonial-style Rockwall Farm was built in 1854 by Tom Harris just west of what became Longview. The house for a time served as an overnight stage stop. The structure burned in 1952.

COURTESY OF THE GREGG COUNTY HISTORICAL MUSEUM.

game, and the Cherokees figured they wouldn't be bothered anymore by the government.

To mark their way in the virgin pines, they cleared a path by felling trees, removing underbrush and planting roses and honeysuckle along this early-day thoroughfare that became known as the Cherokee Trace. A portion of that famous trail passed through what today is Gregg County, which housed a Cherokee community called Big Head Village. Sam Houston and David Crockett reportedly traveled the trace on their way south to Nacogdoches.

But as thousands of American settlers streamed into East Texas, they required more land. Conflicts arose, and the conflicts developed into open hostility and acts of violence by both sides.

By 1839, following the bloody Battle of the Neches in Smith and Van Zandt Counties, the Cherokees had been driven from East Texas and into Oklahoma's Indian Territory. Twenty years later, the remaining Caddoes were resettled in Oklahoma.

SMALL FARMS & PLANTATIONS

As East Texas was settled, many small farms and some plantations began to dot the landscape. The majority of new arrivals came from the Southern United States, some bringing slaves with them. Cotton was, of course, the area's major money crop. Jefferson, on the Big Cypress Bayou, served as the outlet for East Texas cotton. Steamboats from Jefferson plied Caddo Lake and the Red River to Shreveport, Louisiana, and then south to New Orleans.

Between 1836 and 1846 the slave population of Texas increased from some 5,000 to approximately 38,000. By 1856 that count was fifty-eight thousand with the need for laborers to clear the fields, to plant seed and to harvest crops. Many of the slaves were in East Texas.

Only a small portion (3.6 percent) of the state's total population actually owned slaves and few farmers had slaves. The typical farm family did all of the work needed to grow cotton, corn and potatoes. Early settlements usually had cotton gins where the cotton could be ginned and baled. The corn was ground into cornmeal at grist mills.

As more people arrived, villages emerged and churches began to be founded. Prior to 1836, when Texas won its independence from Mexico, Protestant denominations were restricted in their activities. Roman Catholicism was the only religion recognized by the Mexican government.

After independence, denominations grew rapidly in East Texas as religious bodies started to send preachers and other "missionaries" into the area. Pine Tree Cumberland Presbyterian is thought to be the first church established in the Gregg County area. It was founded in 1847 and remains one of the oldest churches in continuous service in Texas.

No system of public education existed when Texas became a state in 1845. Even with passage of a permanent school fund, few public schools were established prior to the 1860s. What today is the Pine Tree Independent School District actually began in 1847, meeting in a log building owned by the aforementioned Pine Tree Cumberland Presbyterian Church.

EARLY COMMUNITIES

One of the earliest settlements in present-day Gregg County was Camden (originally called Walling's Ferry), located on the south side of the Sabine River near today's Easton community. Travelers from Jefferson and Marshall crossed the Sabine at the ferry site operated by John Walling. The village eventually featured several stores, a Presbyterian church, hotel, saloons, a Masonic Lodge and a jug factory.

For a number of years, river boats plied the Sabine to Camden, whose importance was indicated when it was included on the route of one of Texas' earliest telegraph lines in 1854. The village began to decline shortly after the Civil War.

Another early village was Fredonia, a community located at what today is Interstate 20 and FM 2087. It, too, was a river port. Fredonia was home to 40 or 50 buildings including dwellings, a brick kiln and cotton warehouses. The town prospered but by the 1870s declined when it was bypassed by the railroad...a fate suffered by many early East Texas settlements.

Earpville (pronounced "Arpville") was a community lying along the Marshall-Tyler Stagecoach Road (now U.S. Highway 80). The road, a narrow red-clay trail, connected Shreveport, Louisiana, with points west and was a major thoroughfare for people coming into Texas.

In 1848, James Earp bought one-thousand-plus acres which today cover east and central Longview. A stagecoach stop and post office were established and other businesses soon followed. Farming was the main occupation of residents but the town also boasted three merchants, a saddler, carpenter, three blacksmiths and a wagon maker. Near the stagecoach stop, various denominations began meeting in a new frame church building erected by local Methodists.

With westward expansion of the railroad from Marshall and Hallsville to the new village

Mr. and Mrs. O. H. Methvin, Sr. In 1870, O. H. Methvin (1815-1882) gave one hundred acres to the Southern Pacific Railroad (later Texas & Pacific) to found the new village of Longview. The Methvin home was on Rock Hill, sometimes called Methvin Hill, where the town reportedly got its name because of a "long view" from the summit.

COURTESY OF THE GREGG COUNTY HISTORICAL MUSEUM.

Below: This early Gregg County family was ready for another hard-day's work. In 1890 there were more than 600 small farms cultivating county land. Among field crops were cotton, corn, melons, sorghum, potatoes and fruits.

COURTESY OF THE GREGG COUNTY HISTORICAL MUSEUM.

❖

Above: First Baptist Church, Gladewater, was organized in the late 1840s under the name of Bethel Baptist Church. Along about 1899 the church moved to its present location.

COURTESY OF THE GREGG COUNTY HISTORICAL MUSEUM.

of Longview, Earpville began to fade and lose its identity. Earpville also was hurt by another moniker, "Steal Easy," a name given it by travelers concerned by unsavory characters who lived in the area.

Among other early Gregg County settlements were Bethel, Calhoun, Carter's Mill, Cotton Plant (Iron Bridge), Elderville, Hughey, Killingsworth, New Danville, Omega, Peatown, Phillipi, Pleasant Green (founded by freed slaves), Point Pleasant (Gilead), Rock Springs, Shiloh and Tryon. Bethel was home to an early Baptist congregation in the 1840s that later formed what became Gladewater's First Baptist Church.

'LONG VIEW' FROM ROCK HILL

Longview got its name, the generally accepted tale goes, because when the town site was being laid out there was a tall hill—variously known as Rock Hill or Methvin Hill—from which one had a "long view" of the area below.

It was in 1870 when Ossamus Hitch Methvin deeded land to the Southern Pacific Railroad so the railroad would run a line through the new settlement and build a permanent railroad station. Georgia native Methvin and his wife, Margaret, had lived in the area since the late 1840s. They built a three-story home on Rock Hill. Their corn field was located where the Gregg County Courthouse now sits.

As the story goes, Methvin and the surveyors were standing atop Rock Hill when one of the surveyors remarked about the view. Methvin suggested that "Longview" would be appropriate for the new town.

Rock Hill -- still the highest point in town -- once was much taller than it now is and no doubt provided a spectacular view. The hill has been lowered considerably because many of Longview's early homes and businesses used the hill's rock for foundations and chimneys.

In September 1870 the Methvins conveyed an additional fifty acres to the railroad. Rail officials then proceeded to lay out and plat the tracts into lots and blocks. Streets were 100 feet wide. The Longview post office was established in January 1871 with O. H. Pegues as first postmaster. In May the city was incorporated.

Below: Joseph M. Sparkman (1828-1911) settled in the area in 1861. He operated a shoe factory for the Confederate Army and was first justice of the peace, Precinct 2, when Gregg County was organized.

COURTESY OF THE GREGG COUNTY HISTORICAL MUSEUM.

Bottom, right: Built in 1959 by Dr. J.N. Allison, this beautiful house on Dundee Road was located near the Lathrop well that was the Longview area's first producing well in 1931. The house later came to be called the Dundee Angus Ranch.

COURTESY OF THE GREGG COUNTY HISTORICAL MUSEUM.

Chapter II

It Almost Was Called Roanoke County

Gregg County almost was called Roanoke County. However, efforts of a local preacher-politician resulted in the new East Texas political subdivision being named after a slain Confederate general.

The area now known as Gregg County was a part of Nacogdoches County, one of the original counties of the Republic of Texas. Then, in 1846, Upshur County was created from parts of Nacogdoches and Harrison Counties. By the early 1870s, local folks grew tired of having to travel all the way to Gilmer, the Upshur County seat, to transact official business. That's when they petitioned the administration of Texas Governor Edmond J. Davis to carve out a new East Texas county.

The idea was taken up by the Texas Legislature and then somebody came up with the idea of calling the proposed county Roanoke. Exactly why Roanoke was suggested appears to be a mystery. There is speculation that former Virginians recommended the name to honor the community back in their home state. However, the Reverend B. W. Brown, a Methodist-Episcopal Church minister and Upshur County representative in the Thirteenth Texas Legislature, said the county should be named after the late General John Gregg, who had died in the Civil War while leading his men in battle.

Gregg, an Alabama native, had been a mathematics and language instructor. He became a lawyer and in 1852 moved to Texas. He served at the 1860 Secession Convention and was one of Texas'

Joe L. Still (second from left) and several workers stand in front of one of the locomotives serving on county rails at the turn of the century.

COURTESY OF THE GREGG COUNTY HISTORICAL MUSEUM.

representatives to the Confederacy's Provisional Government. He resigned, however, enlisting in the Seventh Texas Regiment as a colonel. Captured by Union troops and later exchanged, Gregg continued to fight in the war and was a brigadier general at the time of his death. He was only thirty-six years old when he died in Virginia in October 1864.

State Representative Brown got the Legislature to rename the county. In April 1873 legislators passed the act authorizing Gregg County, which was created from a part of Upshur County. The act became law the following month.

Right: The county is named for Confederate Gen. John Gregg, who was killed in the Civil War at age thirty-six. The Alabama native was a Texas district judge and a leader in the state's secessionist movement.

COURTESY OF THE GREGG COUNTY HISTORICAL MUSEUM.

AWALT LOSES OUT IN AN ELECTION

Surveyor Andrew S. Taylor was appointed to run the lines of the new county, which he did for three dollars a mile. The new county ran from the southeast corner of Upshur County south to the middle of the Sabine River. Because the original act mandated that the line not come any closer than twelve miles to Gilmer, in 1882 a small portion of Gregg's northern boundary was returned to Upshur County.

Gregg was, and remains with a land area of 274 square miles (according to the Texas Almanac), one of the smallest counties in Texas. Originally Gregg was to be much larger—consisting of at least nine hundred square miles with land from Harrison, Upshur and Rusk counties. However, Harrison County representatives were successful in preventing the western portion of their county from being moved into Gregg. (At the time, Harrison was one of the most populated, politically powerful counties in the state.)

The Reverend Brown is a story in himself. Brown, whose grandfather had been a military engineer under Napoleon Bonaparte, served three terms in the Texas Legislature. He was a delegate to three state Democratic conventions and served on the commission that located the East Texas penitentiary at Rusk. The man we can credit with naming Gregg County died January 9, 1897, and is buried in Longview's Greenwood Cemetery.

With a county organized, residents needed to vote on a county seat and elect officers. On June 25, 1873, Gregg Countians started casting ballots for Longview or Awalt (an area west of Longview later called Willow Springs) to be the seat of government. Awalt had been named for Solomon Awalt, a preacher.

Longview, which carried the election 524 votes to 125 for Awalt, won out for a couple of reasons. One, Longview was bigger. Two, the Texas and Pacific Railroad (successor to the Southern Pacific) had agreed to donate land in Longview for the necessary county offices.

John Witherspoon was selected county judge, R. B. Levy was elected district clerk and

Below: The Reverend B. W. Brown family. Brown, a Methodist lay preacher and state legislator, helped create a new East Texas county and suggested that it be named Gregg County. The family home was located at 104 W. Whaley Street in Longview, and today is known as the Brown-Birdsong home.

COURTESY OF THE GREGG COUNTY HISTORICAL MUSEUM.

M. L. Durham the county's first sheriff. Elected commissioners were T. D. Campbell, J. M. Sparkman, John W. Lawrence, W. H. Payne, and W. P. Victory.

According to a 1928 county history by Rosa Richkie, 50,000 feet of lumber and 20,000 shingles were set aside for construction of the new courthouse, which was ready for occupancy by September 1873 with District Judge A. B. Morton presiding. Soon the county set about building a jail and public roads to accommodate Gregg County's new settlement.

County officials also petitioned the state to increase the subdivision's area. In April 1874, the Texas Legislature formally extended the boundaries south of the Sabine River into a portion of Rusk County, basically doubling Gregg County's land area.

COMING OF THE RAILROADS

Longview was the western terminus for the Texas and Pacific. By 1873 work had started toward constructing the T&P tracks west to Dallas.

In December 1872, Jarrett Dean and Anderson White conveyed to the Texas & Pacific—each for $5—right of way to survey and lay out a new community that would be named Gladewater. In May 1873 the first train rolled into Gladewater. The community incorporated in 1874 with W. D. Thompson named mayor.

The International & Great Northern in 1872 had reached Longview Junction, a small commercial and residential center just east of Longview.

Oxen teams laden with cotton deposited more than one hundred thousand bales annually at the Longview railhead. Then the cotton was transported by rail to Shreveport for shipment via steamers to New Orleans, Louisiana. With the railroad came tremendous growth, not all of it necessarily progress. Pioneer businessman Oliver Pegues, who rode the first train from Hallsville to Longview in 1871, recalled that "enterprising residents opened 32 saloons" in preparation for the business the iron horses would bring.

Many of the establishments sported "gambling dens." One early account noted that merchants often told their lady clerks "to leave the stores at noon, because there were so many drunkards around town in the afternoon."

Countering the "dens in iniquity" was establishment of several church congregations, including First Baptist (1871), First Presbyterian (1872), First Methodist (1873, having relocated from Earpville); Trinity Episcopal (1874), Bethel Baptist (1874) and First Christian (1875). In

❖

Above: This Texas & Pacific locomotive was one of many such engines that made Gregg County a railroad center.

COURTESY OF THE GREGG COUNTY HISTORICAL MUSEUM.

Below: The Texas & Pacific "uptown" depot on Fredonia Street was one of two depots that served Longview. A second depot was located at the Junction just east of town.

COURTESY OF THE GREGG COUNTY HISTORICAL MUSEUM.

1880 the Catholic parish of St. Anthony was established with a church being erected by 1884.

Unique among local churches is St. Mark Christian Methodist Episcopal Church, which originated from a brush arbor that was located on the site of Longview's present-day Magrill Plaza, Green and Padon streets. The story goes back to post-Civil War days when John Magrill, a white man, reportedly donated the small tract of land to "all persons of African descent in Upshur County." The area was known as "the groves" and had been a popular gathering spot for ex-slaves who also worshiped at the brush arbor there.

The city of Longview and a garden club maintain the landscaped park, which is home to a beautiful gazebo and for many years housed the city's official Christmas tree.

Although several Jewish families resided in the county, they worshiped with congregations in nearby counties. (Kilgore's Beth Shalom synagogue was formed in 1936 while Longview's Temple Emanu-el wasn't built until 1958.)

With the railroad came tremendous growth. Among Longview's earliest merchants was William George Northcutt, who established Northcutt Hardware and Furniture Co. Twice serving as mayor, Northcutt also owned a marble works and a brickyard where the first bricks in Longview were made.

A son, Dr. William Davis Northcutt, was one of the county's earliest physicians and practiced medicine for forty-five years. He, too, served two terms as mayor. The Northcutts' Victorian family home, built in 1902, still stands on South Fredonia Street. (One of Dr. Northcutt's daughters, Dolly, was named "First Lady of the First Century" when the city celebrated its centennial in 1970.)

Right: The city of Kilgore is named for Constantine Buckley "Buck" Kilgore, who provided land for the new town site. Kilgore was a state senator and longtime U.S. congressman. He is shown with his wife, Fannie.

COURTESY OF THE GREGG COUNTY HISTORICAL MUSEUM.

Below: Gregg County's first "permanent" courthouse building was dedicated in 1879 but was replaced after serving residents for less than two decades.

COURTESY OF THE GREGG COUNTY HISTORICAL MUSEUM.

LAND FROM "BUCK" KILGORE

New Danville thought it was destined to be a rail center, too. The Rusk County town had first been inhabited about 1845. Its founder is considered to be S. Slade Barnett, a Republic of Texas congressman and Rusk County commissioner. New Danville was situated near a former Cherokee Indian village. A Masonic Lodge was started there as was the Gum Spring Presbyterian Church, later becoming First Presbyterian Church of Kilgore.

The New Danville Masonic Female Academy was incorporated in 1854. The school for young women continued to operate there until 1874 when it moved to Kilgore and was renamed Alexander Institute. The school moved in 1894, this time relocating to Jacksonville, Cherokee County. In 1923 the school became known as Lon Morris College, a two-year school affiliated with the United Methodist Church.

When the International & Great Northern Railway Co. extended its line from Longview south toward Palestine in 1872, railroad executives decided to bypass the community of New Danville and plat a new town site just southwest of the village. There was much protest from New Danville but to no avail.

Land for the new town site had been provided by Constantine Buckley "Buck" Kilgore, who later became a state senator and a long-time U.S. congressman. In honor of the land donation, it was decided to call the new townsite Kilgore.

In 1874, thanks to the Texas Legislature, Danville residents found themselves no longer in Rusk County. They had become residents of an expanded Gregg County.

Thomas A. Scott, the new president of the Texas and Pacific Railway, toured East Texas in the early 1870s. Traveling with him was John Wein Forney, a Pennsylvania newspaper publisher and T&P investor. Forney filed stories for his paper back east and gave readers a glimpse of East Texas life:

"Ten miles more carried us to Long View (sic), the end of our 66 miles by rail (from Shreveport). Now we leave the rail for the common road.... Now and then we passed a log cabin, sometimes without shutters to the windows and almost always without glass. Occasionally a fine plantation would look out upon us with a friendly glance, with a cotton planter on the porch surrounded by his neighbors, and when we stopped to water the greeting was cordial, and the inquiries many."

THE LINE REACHES GLADEWATER

The year 1873 saw the Texas and Pacific railroad reach Gladewater, likely named for a nearby stream called Glade Creek. Some residents of St. Clair and Point Pleasant, tiny settlements to the east, moved to Gladewater with the coming of the railroad. In August that year a post office was established at Gladewater.

Gladewater was incorporated in 1874; however, the incorporation soon lapsed. A second attempt at organizing city government was attempted after the turn of the century but that too didn't last long. A new city charter wasn't obtained again until the oil boom of 1931.

Yet another railroad was the ill-fated Longview & Sabine Valley Railway Company, chartered in 1877. The plan was to extend the line south to Carthage and on to the Gulf Coast. However, not everyone supported the enterprise. Said a contemporary newspaper article: "Longview businessmen are afraid the proposed railroad would cut them off from the wagon trade of this section and would have the tendency to build up Carthage and tear down Longview." By 1878 the line had only reached Camden, eleven miles away. In 1886 the railroad's property was deeded to another company.

Above: Alexander Institute, successor to the New Danville Masonic Female Academy founded in 1854, moved to Kilgore in 1873. In 1894 the school relocated to Jacksonville and became Lon Morris College.

COURTESY OF THE GREGG COUNTY HISTORICAL MUSEUM.

Bottom, left: This building housed Longview's Kelly Memorial Methodist Church 1901-1952. It was named for G. A. Kelly who led construction efforts. The church later became First United Methodist Church.

COURTESY OF THE GREGG COUNTY HISTORICAL MUSEUM.

Bottom, right: First Presbyterian Church of Longview, 1900-1940. The church's first building opened in 1874 on land donated by the Texas and Pacific Railroad.

COURTESY OF THE GREGG COUNTY HISTORICAL MUSEUM.

Chapter III

'Age of Energy, Progress & Vigor'

❖

Logging teams from R. G. Brown's lumber company are photographed in front of Longview Commercial College and Lawrence's Corner Drug Store. This photo was taken about 1910.

COURTESY OF THE GREGG COUNTY HISTORICAL MUSEUM.

James Stephen Hogg was only twenty when he arrived in Longview in 1871 to establish the new town's first newspaper. Young Hogg had gotten printer's ink in his blood several years earlier, setting type in his hometown of Rusk. Later he worked at newspapers in Cleburne and Tyler. His widowed sister, Martha, came from Rusk to help him set up equipment for what Hogg called the *Longview News*. From his tiny office opposite the downtown railroad depot, Hogg put out his two-page tri-weekly starting in October. A subscription was $5 annually.

"This is the age of energy, progress and vigor," Hogg told his readers. "Longview must continue to grow more rapidly than it has ever done, and will astonish in its strides to greatness even its best friends." Hogg's Gregg County stay was brief. By December 1871 he'd loaded his printing press on a borrowed wagon and headed to Quitman, Wood County, to establish a paper there.

Hogg became attorney general of Texas by the age of thirty-five. In 1890 he was elected governor, the first native-born Texan to hold the state's highest post.

By 1872 Longview was being served by the *Longview New Era*, followed by the *News Item* in 1873. Other papers that followed over the years included the *Texas New Era*, *Longview Cycle*, *Longview Daily News*, *Gregg County News*, *Longview Clarion*, *Times-Clarion*, and the *Longview Leader*.

In September 1873 a building on Center Street in Longview was designated for use as a courthouse. That structure was replaced by a larger building completed in January 1879 at a cost of $13,447.

While Gregg County hoped to grow and prosper, a yellow-fever epidemic in late 1873 found the county downright inhospitable to outsiders. The disease was sweeping across the South so Mayor J. W. Boring asked the Gregg County Court to consider establishing a quarantine. The court limited the quarantine to residents and trains from Hallsville, Marshall and Shreveport "for a distance of three miles from the corporate limits of each said places." Furthermore, no fruit, goods or merchandise could be delivered or sold in the county. Violators could be fined up to $100 and faced a 30-day jail sentence. Thankfully, the epidemic came and went with little impact locally.

BUILDING IN BRICK & STONE

A much-worse catastrophe occurred in 1877 when much of Longview's central business district burned. Flames broke out at 2 a.m. on Oct. 4 and the fire quickly was fanned by strong winds. John Maddin's Restaurant, a popular gathering place for residents, was the first to go. Then, one by one, other nearby buildings—all built of wood—were consumed.

Bucket brigades were formed (the Longview Volunteer Fire Company wasn't created until 1885) and the downtown depot and businesses near the courthouse square were saved. However, twenty-five structures, more than half of the downtown area, were turned to ashes. Among losses were A. Bernstein Dry Goods, Harrison and Son Druggists, W. F. Perry's grocery, C. F. Witherspoon's drug store, Joe Newman's grocery and Dold's jewelry store. Total loss for the city of 1,000 residents was $100,000. Downtown was rebuilt—using brick and stone this time—and emerged stronger than ever.

One of Gregg County's first tourist attractions was Phillips Springs, developed in 1877 by A. M. Phillips and located near Gladewater. Visitors traveled to the site to bathe in the springs and to partake of the "medicinal qualities" of the water. Phillips built a hotel at the springs but it burned about five years later. (Lake Gladewater, built in the early 1950s, encompasses the former springs.)

In 1878, Gregg County contracted to build a public bridge across Grace Creek, which at the time was a much wider tributary that couldn't be crossed by wagon. From 1873-78 a man named Winne operated a toll bridge across the creek. The county bridge put an end to Winne's thriving enterprise.

By 1880 Gregg County had 8,530 residents. Longview showed a count of 1,525. In addition to the railroad, lumber was important to the county's early economy. At the end of the decade some twenty steam-powered sawmills were operating. Cotton remained the main cash crop followed closely by corn.

Marion County's misfortune was Gregg County's good luck when a fire destroyed the G. A. Kelly plow works near Jefferson. The firm moved here in 1882 and eventually occupied an entire city block between High and Center streets in downtown Longview. It was Longview's first real manufacturing facility and is said to have been Texas' first chartered industry. For many decades the plant turned out its famous "Kelly Blue" turning plows. The firm branched out, producing a variety of agricultural implements.

G. A. Kelly, who died in 1909, left his mark on Gregg County. Active in civic affairs, he even had a church named after him. When the Methodists built a new brick building in 1900-01, the congregation voted to name the church after Kelly, who headed the fund drive and served as architect and contractor. For many years, what today is Longview's First United Methodist Church was called Kelly Memorial Methodist Church.

In 1883, Longview's mule-drawn streetcar, one of the first in Texas, went into operation between the "uptown" T&P depot and Longview Junction's I&GN depot at Sixth and Methvin streets. Putting together the enterprise were local businessmen C.W. Booth, E.H. Carter, George Harrison, R.B. Levy, Dock Pegues, Frank T. Rembert and F.L. Whaley. The Longview and Junction Railway Company began business with a 12-foot-long car pulled by a single mule. One-way fare was a nickel.

Once the car reached the end of the 3,300-foot narrow-gauge line, the operator—for many years the driver was a colorful fellow named "Uncle" Isaac Smith—would unhitch the "singletree" (with mules attached), then reattach it to the car's opposite end so the car could begin the return trip. Along about 1896 a second larger car requiring two mules was ordered. One open-air

Top: James Stephen Hogg founded Longview's first newspaper at age twenty. Hogg later was the first native-born Texan to serve as governor of the state.

COURTESY OF THE GREGG COUNTY HISTORICAL MUSEUM.

Above: Longtime civic leader George Addison "G. A." Kelly located the county's first industry in Longview.

COURTESY OF THE GREGG COUNTY HISTORICAL MUSEUM.

Bottom: G. A. Kelly's business moved to Gregg County from Marion County in 1882. The firm made the famous "Kelly Blue" plow as well as other agricultural implements.

COURTESY OF THE GREGG COUNTY HISTORICAL MUSEUM.

Above: Located at Longview Junction, the impressive Mobberly Hotel opened in 1884 and was operated by Sam H. Mobberly and his son, Sam Jr. The building burned in 1965.

COURTESY OF THE GREGG COUNTY HISTORICAL MUSEUM.

Below: The Longview Cotton Compress went into business in 1909. Cotton was a major crop early in the county's history with a number of gins located in the area.

COURTESY OF THE GREGG COUNTY HISTORICAL MUSEUM.

vehicle was used during summer and spring; a fully enclosed car protected riders in the fall and winter. As many as twenty passengers could ride.

By 1912 the mule-drawn system—reportedly the shortest railway system in the United States—was replaced by an electric railway with a new 16-foot trolley. The trolley operated until 1922, when paved streets and availability of autos made the enterprise obsolete.

AN ELECTION—BUT NO VOTERS

The impressive Mobberly Hotel was built at Longview Junction in 1884, and was considered one of the finest between Dallas and New Orleans. In 1885 the town formed a volunteer fire department.

In 1883 Kilgore-area residents petitioned for a local-option liquor election in their precinct. On a September day election officials opened the polling place and prepared for the rush of voters. But nobody came -- not even the 22 men who'd signed the petition to force the election in the first place. A second election had to be called and that time the prohibitionists carried the day. It was, according to one account, "curtains for John Barley-corn in Kilgore."

J. W. Johnson bought the *Longview Clarion* newspaper in 1888 and published it as the *Times-Clarion* for more than a quarter-century. An unabashed booster of his hometown, he admonished his readers, "Citizens of Longview, are you aware that more towns die for want of confidence on the part of business men and lack of public spirit than from any other causes? Longview wants the Santa Fe shops, a modern school building, a cotton mill and furniture factory, and, if the citizens will only do their duty, she will get them."

When Longview had its own liquor election in 1905, Johnson wryly noted that while anti-liquor meetings were opened with prayer, the pro-liquor meetings "were opened with a corkscrew." Prohibitionists again carried the day, 883 votes to 733.

With increased population came the need to educate the growing number of children. In 1893 the Gregg County Commissioners Court divided the county into 11 school districts, each with a board of trustees. The county judge served as ex-officio school superintendent at first. The initial county school superintendent was J. Henry Smith of Gladewater, who assumed the post in 1906.

Through the years several of the tiny districts consolidated. One was the Valley Home School District which came to be called Gladewater County Line Independent School District.

Growth in the Spring Hill community northwest of Longview saw a school built there in 1887. A decade later a new building was erected with the first floor for church services and the top floor housing the school. The school evolved into what today is the Spring Hill Independent School District.

THE DALTON BANK ROBBERY

On May 23, 1894, Bill Dalton (of the infamous Dalton outlaw brothers) and three

cronies rode into Longview and robbed the First National Bank. More than 200 shots reportedly were fired in the resulting gunfight that saw one bandit and two townspeople killed. Several residents were wounded, including City Marshal Matt Muckleroy. An outlaw's bullet struck the lawman in the chest but was deflected by a silver coin Muckleroy carried in a coin purse in his pocket.

The gang hightailed it out of town and eventually made its way to Indian Territory. Dalton and a gang member were tracked down and killed by posse members; the remaining outlaw eventually was captured and sentenced to prison.

Surprisingly, Gregg County had several encounters with Old West desperadoes through the years. In addition to the Dalton bank robbery, gunfighter John Wesley Hardin reportedly committed one of Longview's first murders in 1871. Cole Younger even came to town, fortunately only to give a lecture at the Longview Opera House after his outlaw days had ended. In the 1940s J. Frank Dalton, who later claimed to be Jesse James, lived in Longview. "Brushy Bill" Roberts, who gained notoriety by claiming to be William "Billy the Kid" Bonney, called Gladewater home at the same time.

Top, left: Bill Dalton and his outlaw gang robbed Longview's First National Bank on May 23, 1894. Two townspeople and one bandit died in the shootout with several other residents wounded.

COURTESY OF THE GREGG COUNTY HISTORICAL MUSEUM.

Above: The Longview Public School class of May 1899 included Mack Lamar, Brownie Prothro, Noel Mobberly, Margaret Levy, John Brown, B. W. Crain, Sr., Kathlene Howard, Manie Brown, Annie Bob Brown, Lucetta Butts, Betty Mae Oliver, Flo Bramlette, Harvey Van Orden, Junius Flewellen, John Morrow, and Laurence Chaney.

COURTESY OF THE GREGG COUNTY HISTORICAL MUSEUM.

Left: The first organized school for black students in Longview, a four-room frame structure, was constructed in 1888. A modern high school, later called Mary C. Womack High, was built in 1948.

COURTESY OF THE GREGG COUNTY HISTORICAL MUSEUM.

Chapter IV

Wheeler-Dealers & Big-Wigs

❖

These Gregg County farmers proudly show off their produce a century ago in downtown Longview. At left is old city hall and fire station.

COURTESY OF THE GREGG COUNTY HISTORICAL MUSEUM.

In 1896, Frank T. Rembert was elected mayor of Longview. Rembert might be described as the city's first wheeler-dealer. He was a banker, cotton buyer and sports enthusiast, for a while operating a popular horserace track. He owned the first automobile in town (a 1910 Buick) and for decades played a leading role in the development of Gregg County. He also was said to be Longview's first millionaire.

Moving to town in the late 1870s, Rembert married Kate Womack of Marshall and opened the Rembert Mercantile Company. Soon he owned all the buildings along a one-block area of South Fredonia Street known for years as the "Rembert block." In 1908 he built the Palace Hotel and a few years later constructed the Rembert Theater next door. He and others bought the Guaranty State Bank, later called the Rembert National Bank.

The Remberts journeyed to Europe where he was enthralled by a Scottish lake, Loch Lomond. Inspired, Rembert—with fellow investors Robert F. Echols and Hugh Echols—returned to Gregg County and built a lake of his own west of Longview in 1909-1910. For years it was a swimming and boating area as well as a popular gathering place for residents. The lake is located just south of U.S. 80 and west of what today is called Lake Lamond Road.

Investors led by Judge J. N. Campbell created another lake, Devernia, east of Gladewater, in 1914. The lake reportedly was named for Campbell's mother and daughter. The lake area proved to be quite valuable when the oil boom hit East Texas in the 1930s. More than fifty wells were producing on the lake property.

Another prominent businessman was Lafayette Johnson "L. J." Everett. He owned the first horseless carriage in Gladewater, where he opened a mercantile store in 1888. He acquired several businesses, farm property and a sawmill. In 1904, Everett helped organize the Citizens National Bank of Longview

and became its president. In 1910 Everett built a new bank structure, designed by architect Samuel Blocker, at Fredonia and Bank Streets.

Through the years the Everett Building housed several banks and businesses. In 1979 Ann Lacy Crain presented the building to the Gregg County Historical Foundation. After restoration, the new Gregg County Historical Museum opened to the public in 1984. The building at 214 North Fredonia Street is the city's only example of classical revival commercial architecture. It is designated a Registered Texas Historic Landmark and is on the National Register of Historic Places.

Influential Gregg County politicians of the time included C. B. "Buck" Kilgore, elected a U.S. congressman in 1887, and Reese Calhoun DeGraffenried, who in 1896 defeated Kilgore to represent the Third District in Washington, D.C. Kilgore, a Confederate cavalryman during the Civil War, served four terms in Congress and was quite a colorful character.

Perhaps Kilgore's best-remembered congressional act took place in 1890 when the Speaker of the U.S. House locked the doors to the U.S. House of Representatives in Washington, D.C. As the minority party at the time, Kilgore's fellow Democrats had a history of not answering "here" when a roll call was taken in the chamber. Kilgore, however, proclaimed, "Unlock that door. Make way for liberty!" and proceeded to kick open the chamber door with a loud thud. The door swung open—right into the nose of Maine Rep. Nelson Dingley, a former governor of that state.

The feisty Kilgore later was appointed a U.S. judge in Oklahoma Indian Territory. He died in 1897 and was buried in his adopted home of Wills Point.

"BLACK HAWK" & "COLONEL BODIE"

DeGraffenried, known as the "Black Hawk," quickly became a popular figure in the nation's

Top, left: Lafayette Johnson Everett, who owned Gladewater's first auto, helped organize the Citizens National Bank in Longview in 1904 and was its first president. The Gregg County Historical Museum today is housed in the former bank building.

COURTESY OF THE GREGG COUNTY HISTORICAL MUSEUM.

Above: The L. J. Everett home in Gladewater. Everett was a longtime banker, mercantile owner and civic leader in the county.

COURTESY OF THE GREGG COUNTY HISTORICAL MUSEUM.

Left: The Everett Building, 214 North Fredonia Street, Longview, was completed in 1910 by L. J. Everett. Noted architect Samuel J. Blocker designed the building, which in 1979 was presented to the Gregg County Historical Foundation by Ann Lacy Crain. Since 1984 the Everett Building has been home to the Gregg County Historical Museum.

COURTESY OF THE GREGG COUNTY HISTORICAL MUSEUM.

❖

Above: Known as the "Black Hawk" for his oratory skills, Reese C. DeGraffenried served three terms as a U.S. congressman until his death in 1902 in Washington, D.C.

COURTESY OF THE GREGG COUNTY HISTORICAL MUSEUM.

Top, right: Thomas M. Campbell was the county's second resident to become governor of Texas. His childhood friend James Stephen Hogg also was elected the state's chief executive.

COURTESY OF THE GREGG COUNTY HISTORICAL MUSEUM.

Below: Gabriel Augustus "Bodie" Bodenheim served as Longview mayor for some twenty years after the turn of the century. The colorful mayor's trademarks were a gold-headed cane and a carnation in his lapel.

COURTESY OF THE GREGG COUNTY HISTORICAL MUSEUM.

capital. He was known for his oratory and flowing mustache.

DeGraffenried twice won re-election to Congress, but in August 1902 died unexpectedly in Washington, D.C. He was buried in Longview's Greenwood Cemetery. Services were attended by six thousand people. Every business closed on the day of the funeral.

Prominent in the county's development at this time was Gabriel Augustus Bodenheim, who served almost two decades as Longview's mayor. "Colonel Bodie," as he was known to residents, was a colorful character whose trademarks were a carnation in his lapel and a gold-headed walking cane. Bodenheim led the city during some of its most progressive, and most difficult, times.

Under his leadership the city had its first major expansion of the corporate limits, taking in Longview Junction around 1904. He was instrumental in creating the city's first paid fire department, health department, modern waterworks and sewage systems, first paved streets and a modern "Corinthian Standard" street-lighting system. Mayor Bodenheim also provided strong leadership in 1919 when Longview suffered through a race riot that briefly resulted in martial law being declared in Gregg County.

Beautifully landscaped Bodie Park, located on Tyler Street downtown, honored Bodenheim and was a showplace and popular gathering place for residents for three decades. With discovery of the East Texas Oil Field in the 1930s, Bodie Park gave way to commercial development.

Gregg County also was home to a man who may have built an airplane that flew before the Wright brothers' famous 1903 flight at Kitty Hawk, North Carolina. Reverend Burrell Cannon, a Mississippi native and Baptist preacher, moved to the county in the late 1870s.

He operated a sawmill but was fascinated with flight. In 1900 he began to build an "aeroplane" designed from biblical scripture. The so-called Ezekiel Airship was built in a Pittsburg (Camp County) shop and, according to witnesses, made a successful short flight in 1902. The craft later was destroyed in a storm. Cannon died in Longview in 1922.

In the late 1880s a community grew up around White Oak school. An oil-rich White Oak Independent School District eventually was created after the East Texas Oil Boom of the 1930s.

The turn of the century showed 12,343 people living in Gregg County. Longview's population was 3,591.

PRESIDENT TAFT COMES CALLING

In 1906 a second former resident of Longview became governor of Texas. He was Thomas Mitchell Campbell, ironically a childhood best friend of James Stephen Hogg, founder of Longview's first newspaper and first native-born governor. As a young man Campbell worked in the Gregg County clerk's courthouse office and studied law at night. In 1878 he was admitted to the bar and set up a local law practice. He married Fannie Bruner in 1878 and raised five children.

In 1891 he was appointed receiver for the International & Great Northern Railroad and moved to Palestine, Anderson County. He became the railroad's general manager and then ran successfully for governor. He was re-elected governor in 1908. As governor he reformed the state prison system, initiated railroad-regulation reforms and increased tax support for public education.

Residents were excited in 1909 when Gregg County hosted its first presidential visit. On October 24, President William Howard Taft's train "Mayflower" arrived from Dallas and chugged into Longview's downtown depot, where a crowd of several thousand had gathered. Standing under a twenty-five-foot-tall bunting arch, Taft addressed the gathering and, ever the politician, praised Texas governor and former Longviewite Thomas Campbell.

Sports was also a major news item in 1909. The Longview Cannibals baseball team claimed "the amateur championship of all Texas" by defeating McKinney 2-1 at Brown's Park, finishing with a 54-18 record. For more than 40 years Longview's team was called the Cannibals. Local newspaperman C.B. Cunningham had given the team its unique mascot name in 1895 when he reported the Texas League's San Antonio Missionaries "were eaten up by the Longview Cannibals" in an exhibition contest.

That fall also saw the game of football come to Gregg County. Under the headline "FOOT BALL TEAM," the *Times-Clarion* reported, "Longview, always ahead in the procession, now has a first-class foot ball team composed of the following worthy young men: R. E. Rain, J. R. Rainey, W. G. Zeigler, H. H. Watson, Jeff Watson, E. E. Nunsell, Jack Johnston, Ed Newton, Howell Forman, Tully Scott, E. A. Morgan, Earl McCullough, Henry Gunn, Loyd Joslin, Dan Albright, Searcy Birdsong and S. L. Schwartz."

Marshall accepted an invitation to play the new team: "On Thanksgiving Day there was a fine game of foot ball played at Brown's Park between Longview and Marshall, neither team being able to score…it was a good clean game, hotly contested at times." (Longview and Marshall high schools continue to play annually in what is the state's third-longest continuous rivalry.)

Longview's early football field left something to be desired. "The northern end of the field was thickly populated with rocks and pebbles and this discouraged the visiting teams from working toward that goal," said the LHS yearbook, The Finale.

About that time, *Times-Clarion* Publisher J. W. Johnson put out a sixteen-page special edition extolling the virtues of Gregg County. "There was a time not very far back when a man would have been considered nervy to have settled or invested in Gregg County," he told readers. "Today, home seekers will make no mistake by settling on Gregg County's fertile soil, which can be purchased at reasonable prices and on easy terms."

There were stories on Longview's new $50,000 high-school building (Longview became an independent school district in 1909), G. A. Kelly Plow Works, Northcutt Hardware, Algie Perry Drug, Perkins Bros. Dry Goods, W. E. Booth Hardware and T. D. Coupland Co., described as "a leading trade emporium popular with all classes of people." Oden's Picture Palace offered "New pictures every night. Admission 10 cents to all."

Johnson described Kilgore as "a pretty, picturesque little town of 600 or 700 souls" while Gladewater was a town of 1,000 where "the people are wide awake and energetic."

Gladewater, said another publication in 1910, featured "numerous enterprises in and near the town, and the rapidly developing fruit, forage crops, and livestock industry…. There are seven blocks of modern business houses in the town,

❖

For more than a half-century, Longview's semi-pro and professional baseball teams were known as the Cannibals. The team won its name in 1895 when a reporter told readers the local squad had "eaten up" the San Antonio Missionaries in an exhibition game. This Cannibals photo is from the early 1900s.

COURTESY OF THE GREGG COUNTY HISTORICAL MUSEUM.

Below: Longview High School football team, c. 1916. Longview began playing football in 1909 with a Thanksgiving Day game against rival Marshall.

COURTESY OF THE GREGG COUNTY HISTORICAL MUSEUM.

Right: Longview's First National Bank, which opened in 1912, eventually gave way to a taller structure in the mid-1950s. Note the electric trolleys which were operated by the Longview and Junction Railway Company until 1922.

COURTESY OF THE GREGG COUNTY HISTORICAL MUSEUM.

Below: This view of Longview's Methvin Street shows, from left, the post office, old Hurst Clinic (later KFRO radio), the East Texas Chamber of Commerce building and the Hilton Hotel. The East Texas Chamber was organized in Longview in 1926. First president was R. Marvin Kelly. For many years the organization helped coordinate the work of local chambers in seventy-two East Texas counties.

COURTESY OF THE GREGG COUNTY HISTORICAL MUSEUM.

representing every phase of mercantile life, including two large department stores."

That same year Gregg County almost had its first public hanging since 1878. A large crowd converged on downtown Longview one July morning to view the execution of a condemned murderer. A gallows was built for the deed but at the last minute the Texas governor commuted the prisoner's sentence.

"WAS NARY A HANG" reported the *Times-Clarion*: "Several thousands came from all parts of the surrounding country to witness it—and returned home minus the pleasure, dusty, hot and disgusted."

REMEMBERING THE LOST CAUSE

In November 1910 the Richard B. Levy Chapter of the United Daughters of the Confederacy brought famed orator William Jennings Bryan to Gregg County for a lecture. The fifty-cent admission would help the UDC fund a monument to honor Civil War veterans. Bryan (unsuccessful Democratic presidential candidate in 1896, 1900, and 1908) was given a reception at the Magnolia Hotel, then taken to the Longview Opera House which was filled to overflowing.

Bryan's lecture, titled "The Prince of Peace," touched "that chord of good in every heart, stirring the soul to its depths and lifting it to the plane of noble thought and high ideals," reported a local newspaper. Thanks in part to money raised by Bryan's appearance, in June 1911 a Confederate statue was dedicated in Longview's downtown Bodie Park. The statue's unveiling featured a parade, barbecue, motorcycle races, hot-air ascensions, and speeches before revealing of the thirty-five-foot Texas granite-and-Italian marble statue sculpted by Frank Teich.

In 1914, Dr. V. R. Hurst moved to Longview and opened Longview's first hospital-clinic, reportedly the first in the state built exclusively for eye, ear, nose and throat.

Promoting the area was the Longview Chamber of Commerce, founded in 1916, the same year the Kilgore Chronicle was established as the town's first newspaper. The following year many county residents enlisted in the U.S. military to serve in the "Great War."

July 28, 1918, appeared to be another typical humid East Texas day…until the drone of an engine was heard high overhead. Gregg County

was about to be visited by its very first airplane. "Parties in Gladewater had seen the plane go over and had telephoned the news (to Longview) for our people to be on a lookout," the *Times-Clarion* said. "When the plane was first sighted practically every person in Longview was on the door-step watching the sky."

The plane was a C-709 trainer piloted by two Army officers and on its way from Fort Worth to Shreveport, La. Running short of fuel, the plane flew low over downtown and then landed in Utzman's pasture not far from town.

"Immediately, a great stream of cars filled with eager citizens began a violation of the speed laws, city officials joining the chase. The plane was hardly on the ground when great throngs of people were visitors to the spot," reported the paper. Locals got their first close-up look at a real flying machine, which gassed up and lifted "its out-stretched wings to the gentle zephyr breezes…rose higher and yet higher, sailing away in the deep sky above."

Less than a week later, the five-story First National Bank sustained "one of the most disastrous fires" in Longview. Lost were the top floor, which housed the Elks Lodge, and a popular roof garden. The building was repaired but the top floor was so damaged that it was torn away and roofed over. The city's tallest office building went from five stories to four.

PHOTOGRAPHER: NO PLACE TO PLOW

In addition to local newspapers much of Gregg County's history was recorded by photographer Cody Bryant Culpepper, who documented local people and events for more than 50 years. He opened a local studio around 1909 and between 1915 and 1931 was Longview's only photographer.

Asked why he wanted to be a photographer, Culpepper once replied, "Well, I could do two things, take pictures and plow. And I didn't have a place to plow." Fortunately, he chose f-stops over farming. Culpepper died in 1973 at age eighty-four. In 1990, Dr. Norman Black, president of the Gregg County Historical Commission, learned of 309 "lost Culpepper negatives." Receiving Culpepper prints were the Gregg County Historical Museum, the *Longview News-Journal* and Texas Eastman Co., which graciously had the photos reproduced.

By 1917, during the administration of County Judge J. H. McHaney, Gregg County had its first paved road when U.S. 15 (later U.S. 80) received an asphalt treatment. By 1923, the Texas Highway Department was made responsible for building and maintaining a statewide network of highways.

Markham Hospital was founded in Longview by Dr. L. N. Markham—the twenty-five-bed facility operated until the early 1950s—and in 1926 the East Texas Chamber of Commerce was organized with its headquarters at Longview.

Above: Cody and Maude Culpepper enjoy a buggy ride in 1910. Cody Culpepper photographed Gregg County people and activities for five decades.

COURTESY OF THE GREGG COUNTY HISTORICAL MUSEUM.

Below: Cody Culpepper recorded much of Gregg County's history through his lens. He opened a local studio in 1909 and for many years was Longview's only permanent photographer. A number of photos in this book are from the camera of Culpepper.

COURTESY OF THE GREGG COUNTY HISTORICAL MUSEUM.

❖

Top: The Palace Hotel, part of what was called the Rembert downtown block, was owned by Frank T. Rembert. The hotel was at the corner of Fredonia and Cotton Streets in Longview. Rembert was involved in numerous business ventures in the county.

COURTESY OF THE GREGG COUNTY HISTORICAL MUSEUM.

Middle: The John H. Shepperd house, located a mile north of downtown Gladewater, was built in the early 1900s and burned in 1913.

COURTESY OF THE GREGG COUNTY HISTORICAL MUSEUM.

Bottom; The Longview and Junction Railway Company was created in 1883 to operate a mule-drawn trolley between the "uptown" and Junction depots. The mules were replaced by electric cars in 1912. The transit system operated until 1922.

COURTESY OF THE GREGG COUNTY HISTORICAL MUSEUM.

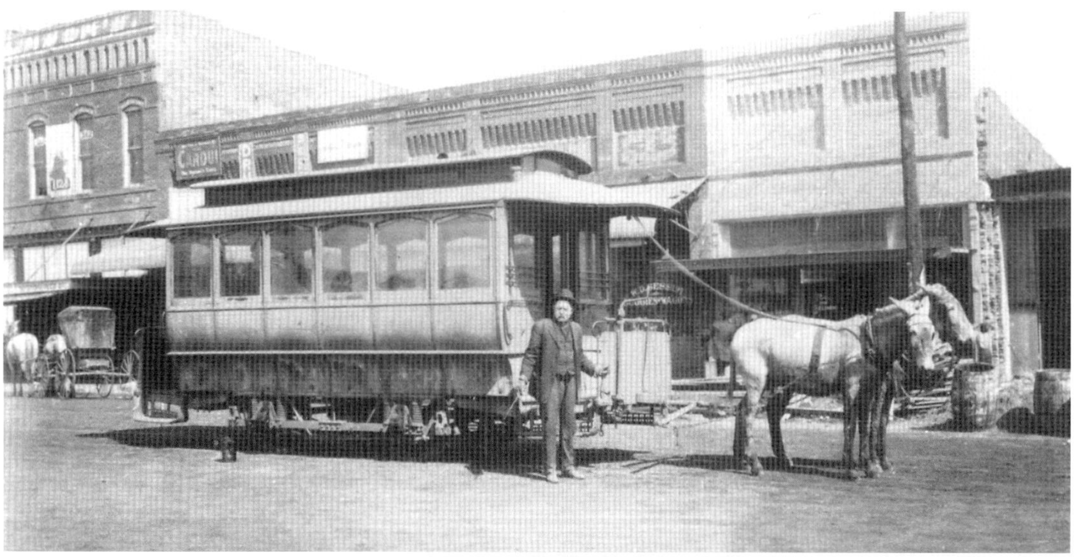

CHAPTER V

A GIANT FIELD OF BLACK GOLD

Prior to the 1929 Stock Market crash and resulting Great Depression, Gregg County suffered its own setback in January of that year when the Texas and Pacific Railway announced it was moving its main terminal from Longview to Mineola. The announcement meant the loss of some 700 T&P employees and their families. The loss of the terminal, many residents and a $1 million payroll was an event from which many residents felt the county would never recover.

High unemployment followed. Then there was a major drought, cotton prices fell, timber production decreased and along came the Depression. It was the worst of times for Gregg County. But it wasn't long before Lady Luck—some said it was divine providence—again smiled on the area.

Back in 1915 an oil well had been drilled near Kilgore. It was a dry hole. However, thanks to C.M. "Dad" Joiner, a seventy-year-old wildcatter and promoter supreme, Gregg County's fortunes were about to change. Joiner had looked for oil in East Texas for years. After a two-year struggle to raise money he drilled a first well on Daisy Bradford's Rusk County farm in 1927 and a second well a year later. Those efforts also failed.

Although some East Texans considered the drilling to be "Joiner's Joke," the third time proved to be the charm. On October 3, 1930, despite a ramshackle derrick driven by a worn-out engine, the Daisy Bradford No. 3 came in a gusher. It was exciting, to be sure, but was the well anything more than an isolated pocket of oil?

❖

Perhaps the most famous picture of the oil boom days: "Dad" Joiner (left) shakes the hand of "Doc" Lloyd at the Daisy Bradford No. 3, the discovery well of the great East Texas Oil Field.

COURTESY OF THE GREGG COUNTY HISTORICAL MUSEUM.

Above: B. A. "Barney" Skipper, checking a core-test sample, tried for years to get oil companies to drill in Gregg County. His efforts paid off in January 1931 when the Lathrop No. 1 well came in north of Longview.
COURTESY OF THE GREGG COUNTY HISTORICAL MUSEUM.

Below: B. A. "Barney" Skipper, left, and F. K. Lathrop, right, flank an unidentified driller at one of the wells they drilled during the oil boom.
COURTESY OF THE GREGG COUNTY HISTORICAL MUSEUM.

Three months later a second well, the Lou Della Crim No. 1, came in on December 28, 1930, southwest of Kilgore. A contemporary newspaper report said the well "opens up a new field 10 to 15 miles along the Sabine uplift, bringing oil to the very door of Gregg County."

On January 26, 1931—almost two years to the day that T&P announced its terminal move—the F. K. Lathrop No. 1 well blew in near Longview. "The well came in as a gusher, strong gas pressure forcing oil over the top of the derrick," said one newspaper account. "A crowd estimated at more than 15,000 persons saw the well come in."

The Longview Chamber of Commerce had promised $10,000 for the first producing well brought in within a dozen miles of town.

For a quarter-century B. A. "Barney" Skipper, a real-estate man and cotton buyer, had been trying to interest oil companies in drilling in the area. He finally worked out a deal with John E. Farrell and W. A. Moncrief to drill the well that proved to be successful. The well was on the farm of Lathrop, manager of the G. A. Kelly Plow Company.

It was the Longview well that confirmed the existence of the world's largest oil field … a field 42 miles long and eight miles wide. It would be called the East Texas Oil Field. In April Gladewater got its first gusher.

THE BOOM IS ON

Within weeks thousands came to East Texas—geologists, petroleum engineers, refiners, wildcatters, roughnecks and roustabouts. Pine trees fell and wooden derricks rose by the hundreds, then thousands. Buildings—including a bank—were razed to make way for the wells. Almost overnight Kilgore's 500 residents exploded to 10,000.

"Kilgore is the most seething, wildly excited and booming oil boom town," said W.R. Smith, president of the Oriental Oil Co. of Dallas. "I have been to every oil field in the Southwest since 1918, but this beats them all … the roads are choked with traffic and there is literally standing room only in the town itself." Many new businesses, according to one contemporary report, "were started in tents with dirt floors."

Kilgore incorporated in February 1931 to prepare for the boom, with J. Malcolm Crim elected mayor and Roy H. Laird and Ben Laird selected commissioners. Eventually more than eleven hundred wells would be situated in Kilgore.

The field covered parts of five counties (Gregg, Rusk, Smith, Upshur, Cherokee). The boom brought the dream tales of dirt-poor farmers with oil-rich lands, trading in their old farm trucks for shiny new automobiles to put in the garages of their big new homes. By August 1931 the giant field was producing an unbelievable million barrels of oil a day. While much of the nation had Depression breadlines, Gregg County had pipelines.

New office buildings went up in Kilgore and Longview, along with new homes, churches, commercial buildings and hospitals. One week in May 1932, Longview led the state with $194,065 in construction. (Houston was second at $46,825; Dallas third with $33,122.)

School enrollment soared, requiring new campuses. When oil was discovered, Pine Tree school between Gladewater and Longview had just three teachers and about one hundred students.

Kilgore found itself with 2,600 students enrolled in the 1932-33 academic year, requiring passage of a bond election to meet demand. Voters also approved a new city hall, fire station, and jail dedicated July 4, 1931. By 1933 Kilgore had more than 30 mercantile stores, a dozen drug stores, 10 restaurants, three theatres, eight refineries, 25 oil-well supply firms and 35 machine shops.

Clubs and honky-tonks sprang up in the county to meet the entertainment needs of oil-field workers. One of the most popular was Mattie's Ballroom between Kilgore and Longview. During its heyday, such musicians as Henry "Satchmo" Armstrong and Jack Teagarden and his orchestra played at Mattie's. The club evolved into a Gregg County landmark called the Reo Palm Isle which could accommodate fifteen hundred dancing couples and featured "the largest, best and most popular orchestras and musical organizations in the country."

"MAIN STREET OF AMERICA"

Highway 15 was widened and soon became U.S. 80, the "Main Street of America." However, most other county roads remained primitive with dirt or gravel surfaces. East Texas had more than its share of rainstorms when the oil boom started, turning the busy roads into quagmires. Driving from Gladewater to Kilgore could take several hours because of the road conditions.

But the field changed life for generations of East Texans and made Gregg County the greatest oil-producing county anywhere.

Kilgore became world famous for its skyline of derricks. By January 1932, Gladewater had 90 producing wells within its corporate limits with more on the way. Even cemeteries prospered. Gladewater's Rosedale Cemetery, which offered burial permits rather than lots (thereby keeping surface and mineral rights to remain with the cemetery association), was the site of well drilling which allowed the association to build a caretaker's cottage, rock fence, roads and landscaping. It was for a time known as the "world's richest self-supporting cemetery."

Above: A sleepy village prior to discovery of oil, Kilgore was transformed almost overnight by the boom.

COURTESY OF THE GREGG COUNTY HISTORICAL MUSEUM.

Bottom, left: Skelly Oil was one of almost one hundred refineries that located in the East Texas Oil Field. The refineries used crude oil to produce gasoline and other petroleum-based products.

COURTESY OF THE GREGG COUNTY HISTORICAL MUSEUM.

Below: Oil-well fires could be deadly, as was this April 1931 blaze near Gladewater. A spark caused by tool friction resulted in an inferno that claimed nine lives.

COURTESY OF THE GREGG COUNTY HISTORICAL MUSEUM.

❖

Top: Martin Hays was elected Longview's city marshal in 1910 and from 1924-1932 served as Gregg County sheriff. He rarely carried a weapon on the job.

COURTESY OF THE GREGG COUNTY HISTORICAL MUSEUM.

Middle: Carl L. Estes was known for his fiery front-page editorials in the Longview News-Journal, *which he bought in 1934. Estes' wife, Margaret, became publisher upon his death in 1967. The* News-Journal *was sold to Cox Enterprises, Inc. in 1978.*

COURTESY OF THE LONGVIEW NEWS-JOURNAL.

Bottom: Charles K. Devall (left) served as publisher of the Kilgore News Herald *from 1935-1979. Through his award-winning paper and civic endeavors, he was a tireless supporter of what he called "America's No. 1 Small City" until his death in January 1995 at the age of eighty-six. He is shown presenting a gift of stock valued at $500,000 to Kilgore College President B. E. Woodruff in 1991. Devall's wife, Lyde Williford Devall (1909-1986), was a University of Texas regent and served on the Texas Commission on Higher Education.*

COURTESY OF KILGORE COLLEGE.

A number of small communities were created because of oil production, including Clarksville City (where St. Clair had been located), Crews, Shell Camp, Swamp City and Teneryville where the Lathrop oil well blew in.

As oil production continued to soar, however, the price of a barrel of oil dropped from just under a dollar to six cents. When the state ordered proration (setting a limit on production based on market demand), lawsuits and injunctions followed. In August 1931 the overproduction caused Gov. Ross Sterling to declare martial law in the oil field.

Hundreds of National Guardsmen, accompanied by Texas Rangers, descended on the oil patch to ensure the wells were shut down. Among those Rangers was the legendary Manuel T. "Lone Wolf" Gonzaullas. Since Kilgore didn't have a jail, Gonzaullas would march lawbreakers to an abandoned church building and secure them to a long chain which came to be called "Lone Wolf's Trotline."

Order was restored and the field resumed production in September 1931. Gonzaullas resigned his Ranger commission in 1933 and ran unsuccessfully for Gregg County sheriff.

To keep up with the unprecedented growth, in March 1932, Gregg County voters approved a $1.5-million bond issue to provide the county 122 miles of roads and 60 miles of state highways. In November that year Longview opened the new Nicholson Memorial Library. Mr. and Mrs. W. R. Nicholson funded construction of the library in memory of their son, Ronald, who had died at the age of twelve. The library served residents for more than fifty years.

In the early 1930s Conrad Hilton bought the 64-room Gregg Hotel in downtown Longview. He promptly renamed it the Longview Hilton, which he doubled in size in 1937. The hotel turned out to be Hilton's inspiration to create one of the largest hotel chains in the world. Hilton was $500,000 in debt and near bankruptcy when Dr. V. R. Hurst of Longview encouraged him to purchase the Gregg.

In his 1957 autobiography Hilton said, "The Longview Hilton was somehow always special to me. Not because it made money. That it did from the start ... But because it stood as my symbol that American business was ready to grow again." Buoyed by his success in Gregg County, Hilton began acquiring other hotels, first in Texas and then around the country. Before long, "Hilton" was the best-known hotel name in the world.

Chapter VI

Baseball, Jack Dempsey & Rangerettes

Prosperity from the East Texas Oil Field even brought Texas League baseball to Gregg County, if for only one season. In May 1932, Shreveport's stadium burned and that team hastily arranged a game at Longview. A big crowd attended, impressing Texas League officials. The Wichita Falls franchise wasn't drawing very well so its parent club, the St. Louis Browns, decided the oil-boom town of Longview might be a good home for its struggling farm club. In late May the Wichita Falls team relocated to Longview. Despite having a fine hitter named Debs Garms (he led the National League in hitting in 1940 with a .355 batting average for the Pittsburgh Pirates), Longview finished with a losing record. Texas League officials moved the club after only one year.

Longview continued in professional ball for a number of years thereafter. In 1933 Longview competed in the Dixie League against such opponents as Waco and Baton Rouge, La. By the early 1950s, after a brief stint in the Big State League, pro baseball became only a memory in Longview.

(Longview was a part of the old East Texas League as early as 1923; Kilgore joined in 1931 and Gladewater by 1935. Minor league baseball continued in the county until the early 1950s.)

Perhaps the finest baseball player to come out of Gregg County was Samuel Filmore "Sammy" West, born in Longview in 1904. A left-handed outfielder, he played 16 years in the major leagues (with the Washington Senators and St. Louis Browns). He set an American League record in 1928 with a .996 fielding average (only one error all season) and was selected to play in the first-ever Major League All-Star Game in Chicago.

A frequent visitor to the county during the oil boom was Jack Dempsey, the former heavyweight boxing champion of the world known as the "Manassa Mauler." Dempsey was involved in several oil deals. Drawing a capacity crowd to referee a wrestling match in 1934, Dempsey told his admirers, "I can't dance and I can't sing. But like the Irishman, to be a good fellow, I will fight anybody in the house." There were no takers.

Longview dedicated a municipal airport in June 1933 with plane races, music and a dance. L.H. Pitkin, a Houston oilman who had built the field 15 months earlier for his own use, gave the dedicatory speech and formally turned the field over to City Manager Bill N. Taylor.

❖

Kilgore College's "Old Main" building opened in November 1936 and remains a landmark on the campus. It served as the school's administration building for many years.

COURTESY OF THE GREGG COUNTY HISTORICAL MUSEUM.

AN OIL PATCH COLLEGE TOWN IS BORN

In 1935 the Texas Board of Education approved creation of a junior college district within the Kilgore Independent School District, and voters approved the creation in July. "Kilgore is backing this college 100 per cent," said the *Kilgore Daily News*. "This college was seriously needed and the people of the Oil Belt are going to show their appreciation by sending their boys and girls to it for their first two years of training."

Kilgore College opened for classes on Sept. 13, 1935, with 229 students enrolled. For the next 11 years the college operated under the KISD's board of trustees with W. L. Dodson as superintendent. In 1946, B. E. Masters became president of the college and eventually other districts joined KISD in the Kilgore College district, including Leverett's Chapel, Sabine, White Oak, London, Overton, Gaston and Gladewater. (Kilgore College opened a satellite campus in Longview in 1979. By the fall semester of 2005, the two-year community college boasted total enrollment of some 5,000.)

The Kilgore College Rangerettes, perhaps Gregg County's best-known goodwill ambassadors, debuted on Sept. 19, 1940, at the halftime of a football game between Kilgore and Daniel Baker College. Organizing the nation's first halftime dance-drill team was Gussie Nell Davis, who served as director until her retirement in 1979. The *Kilgore Daily News* noted the Rangerettes' initial performance—complete with fireworks—was "stunningly beautiful…they pirouetted, pranced, danced in perfect unison, colorful in movement and attire."

Above: Gussie Nell Davis was founder and first director of the world-famous Kilgore College Rangerettes, which performed for the first time on September 19, 1940. She directed the Rangerettes until her retirement in 1979.

COURTESY OF KILGORE COLLEGE)

Since that 1940 debut the Rangerettes—in their trademark red, white and blue uniforms—have performed around the world and appeared on the covers of *Newsweek*, *Texas Monthly*, Look, the *Saturday Evening Post*, and other publications.

In 1935, Charles K. Devall established *The Kilgore Herald*. Five years later he bought a rival paper, the *Daily News*, and his paper became The *Kilgore News Herald*. Devall, publisher until 1979 when he sold the paper, was a tireless supporter for what he called "America's No. 1 Small City." In 1991 Devall presented stock valued at $500,000 to Kilgore College for a new student center. The veteran newspaperman died in 1995.

The boom continued to change Kilgore from a village to a city. In 1936, reported a newspaper, "the new Hotel Kilgore was opened

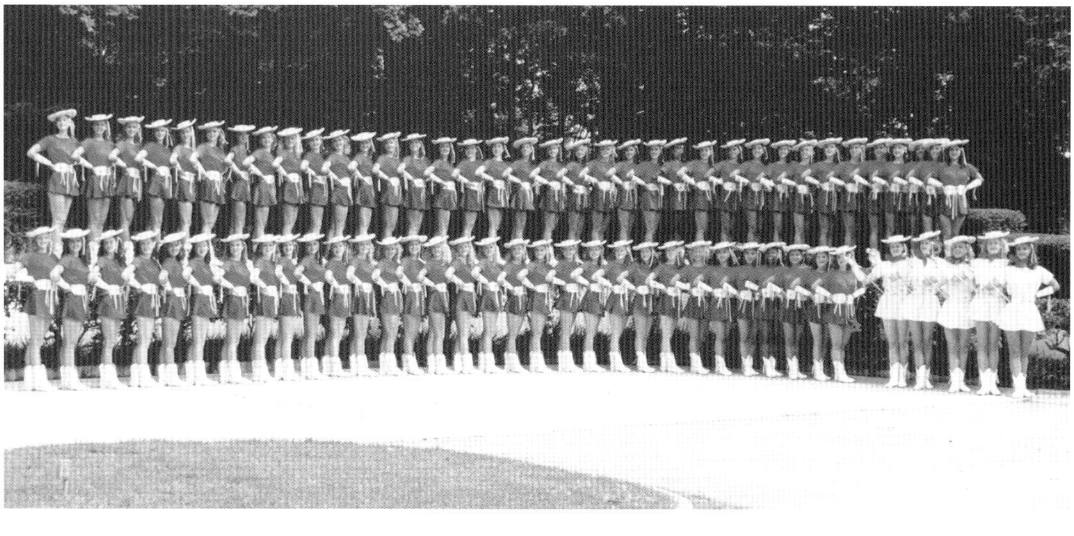

Below: In 1940 the Kilgore College Rangerettes changed football halftimes forever with the nation's first women's dance-drill team. Shown is the 1996-97 Rangerette line.

COURTESY OF KILGORE COLLEGE.

recently; a new natatorium was opened with 706 persons enjoying a plunge the first day; the Meadowbrook Country Club recently opened its commodious new clubhouse; a new hospital, modern in every detail, recently has been opened…foundation has been completed for the Christian Church, ground has been broken for a Catholic Church and a site has been bought for the contemplated Jewish synagogue."

In 1935 the forty-seven-bed Gregg Memorial Hospital opened on Marshall Avenue in Longview. The hospital was enlarged several times through the years and later came to be called Good Shepherd Medical Center. Today the 412-bed facility is a regional referral center.

The Longview Civic Music Association's first membership drive netted 450 members in an effort "to bring high-class concerts to Longview." Gregg County also got its first radio station, KFRO (1370 AM), owned by J.R. Curtis Sr.

That same year a group of American League players led by Rogers Hornsby played an exhibition game against area all-stars. The major leaguers won 9-0. Moviegoers at the time could view the latest flicks at the Rita, the Rembert, the Strand, Liberty, Aladdin and Ritz theaters. Shortly thereafter, Jay Hanna "Dizzy" Dean pitched in an exhibit at Fair Park. "He pitched as beautiful a brand of ball as the customers could ask for," said a newspaper account, noting the "bragging, boasting Dean…struck out seven batters, collected himself a hit, stole three bases and made one sacrifice."

While oil brought untold prosperity, it also brought occasional danger in the form of well blowouts. Typical was this incident reported in November 1935: "GLADEWATER—An oil well only three blocks off the main street blew out of control as it was drilled early Thursday night and ran wild, with thousands of barrels of oil hourly flowing into a nearby creek. Refineries in the vicinity…were ordered shut down and all open fires were prohibited on account of the grave fire hazard created by escaping oil and gas."

For the Texas Centennial of 1936, the Longview Chamber of Commerce erected a large billboard near Texarkana, 90 miles to the north, to attract visitors to U.S. 15 (today U.S. 80), calling the thoroughfare "The East Texas Scenic Highway." The state highway department had begun rebuilding U.S. 15 into a four-lane highway in anticipation of the thousands expected for the year-long centennial events. U.S. 15, for decades the South's main east-west route known as the "Dixie Overland" highway, ran from Savannah, Georgia, to San Diego, California.

What has become one of the state's most popular outdoor rodeos began in 1938 in Gregg County. It is the Gladewater Round-Up Rodeo which annually attracts top professional cowboys and cowgirls. In the first few years the event was held in a makeshift arena built over an earthen pit that had been used to store oil. By 1947 an all-steel arena was constructed, serving rodeo attendees until the rodeo association opened a new five-thousand-seat facility several years ago.

Above: Gregg Memorial Hospital on U.S. 80, Longview, opened as a forty-seven-bed facility in 1935. The hospital later came to be called Good Shepherd Medical Center and is the area's largest medical facility.

COURTESY OF THE GREGG COUNTY HISTORICAL MUSEUM.

Bottom, left: Nicholson Memorial Library was presented to the city of Longview by Mr. and Mrs. W. R. Nicholson in memory of their son. It served book lovers until 1986 when the Longview Public Library was opened.

COURTESY OF THE GREGG COUNTY HISTORICAL MUSEUM.

Bottom, right: This impressive structure at Bank and Fredonia streets opened in 1940 and for two decades housed the Longview National Bank.

COURTESY OF THE GREGG COUNTY HISTORICAL MUSEUM.

❖

Above: The Gladewater Round-Up Rodeo Association annually hosts one of the state's most popular rodeos. The event, which began in 1938, attracts the nation's top professional cowboys and cowgirls. By 1947 an all-steel arena was built to house the event.

COURTESY OF THE GREGG COUNTY HISTORICAL MUSEUM.

A high-school football state championship came to Gregg County in December 1937 when the Longview High School Lobos completed an undefeated season. Led by Coach Pete Shotwell and the Miller brothers, "Dandy" Dick and Hardy, the team went 14-0 and on Christmas Day defeated Wichita Falls 19-12 in the title game at Dallas' Cotton Bowl.

By 1940, thanks to the oil boom, Gregg County's population had grown to 58,027 (from a count of just 15,778 in 1930). Municipal populations included Longview, 13,758; Kilgore, 6,708; and Gladewater, 4,454.

A man responsible for much of the county's growth was *Longview News-Journal* Publisher Carl L. Estes, once described as "like a jet fighter plane; he can't go slow, and the noise he makes is a means toward worthwhile objectives." Estes came to the county from Tyler in 1934 when he bought the Longview newspapers.

He quickly set about securing new industry for the county, actively developed area water resources and became known for his hard-hitting front-page editorials. When he died in 1967, Estes' wife, Margaret, became publisher of the *Longview News-Journal*. A state historical marker calls Carl Estes "one of America's giants of journalism," noting he had "devoted his keen abilities and showman's talents to conserving for human betterment the vast wealth of the East Texas Oil Field."

Another tireless supporter of Gregg County was Syril A. Parker, *News-Journal* president who came to work for the paper in 1928. He served 58 years with the newspaper, which in 1978 was sold to Cox Enterprises, Inc.

THE BEAUTIFUL LACY GARDENS

One of Gregg County's favorite tourist areas for a number of years was Lacy Gardens. For 10 years, beginning in 1939, springtime in East Texas meant a trip to the Lacy home on the Kilgore highway just outside Longview. The gardens were the brainchild of Rogers Lacy, well-known philanthropist and oil-and-gas man who had organized and was first president of Longview's Southern Gas Company.

He founded the R. Lacy Nursery and was considered one of the Southwest's leading fanciers of azaleas and camellias. But he wanted a showcase beauty spot he could share with the world. In 1936 he asked Leonard Riggs, a Louisiana landscape architect and horticulturist, to come to Gregg County to design and build what would be known as the Lacy Gardens. Riggs stayed on as Lacy's nursery superintendent and is credited with introducing the azalea and other rare plants to the area.

Word spread about the gardens and soon the spring flower show—held as part of Longview's "Friendly Trek" home tour—was attracting thousands of visitors. In 1940 the gardens were described this way: "The stately Longview home is surrounded by spacious grounds and beautifully landscaped gardens. Looking from the steps at the back of the home, one sees a marshy brook winding its way through tall pines to a silvery lake upon whose surface glide graceful swans…one sees hundreds of azaleas, irises, lilies, hydrangeas, hyacinths and almost every other kind of flower one can imagine."

Rogers Lacy died in 1947. The following spring marked the final public showing of Lacy Gardens.

Below: The art-deco Crim Theater, opened in 1939 by Liggett Crim and long a downtown Kilgore landmark, is a restoration project of the Kilgore Historical Preservation Foundation.

COURTESY OF THE GREGG COUNTY HISTORICAL MUSEUM.

Chapter VII

East Texas Crude Helps Win the War

With news that Japan had attacked Pearl Harbor on December 7, 1941, patriotic Gregg County residents joined Americans everywhere in joining the military to defeat the Axis powers. Local recruiting stations were swamped. "Scores of men and boys from 17 years of age to as high as 61 crowded into the recruiting offices of the Army, Navy and U.S. Marine Corps all day Monday," said the *Longview Daily News*, noting the Army had so many recruits that application forms had been exhausted.

By December 9 the Longview paper was reporting a "round-up of dangerous aliens in the U.S." Longview Police Chief Albert Adams asked residents to report "subversive, suspicious activities." However, the chief was quick to warn against "malice and hatred of foreign-born persons. Many of our best and most law-abiding citizens are naturalized Americans who love this country above everything else."

The East Texas Rifle and Pistol Club range was opened to the public—just in case—and local officials worried about sabotage in the oil fields. "Blacking out the East Texas Oil Field by night and removal of derricks which would guide enemy bombers by day are two vital needs which should have been foreseen and cannot be accomplished too quickly," said the *Longview Daily News*. "Provision will have to be made for producing the oil by day so that flares will be eliminated after dark."

By December 16, the first casualty reports were coming in from Pearl Harbor: "Mrs. Grace Lee McCranie of Greggton was notified Tuesday morning by the Navy Department in Washington that her son, Billy Bennett Jones, seventeen, former carrier boy for the *News* and *Journal*, was lost in action in performance with his duty in the service of his country." Jones had joined the Navy in August and was sent to Hawaii as an apprentice seaman. He was the first local man to die in the new war. There would be many more.

❖

Located at Longview Junction, this depot for many years was a passenger depot for the Texas & Pacific Railway. Today the depot serves passengers boarding Amtrak's "Texas Eagle" train.

COURTESY OF THE GREGG COUNTY HISTORICAL MUSEUM.

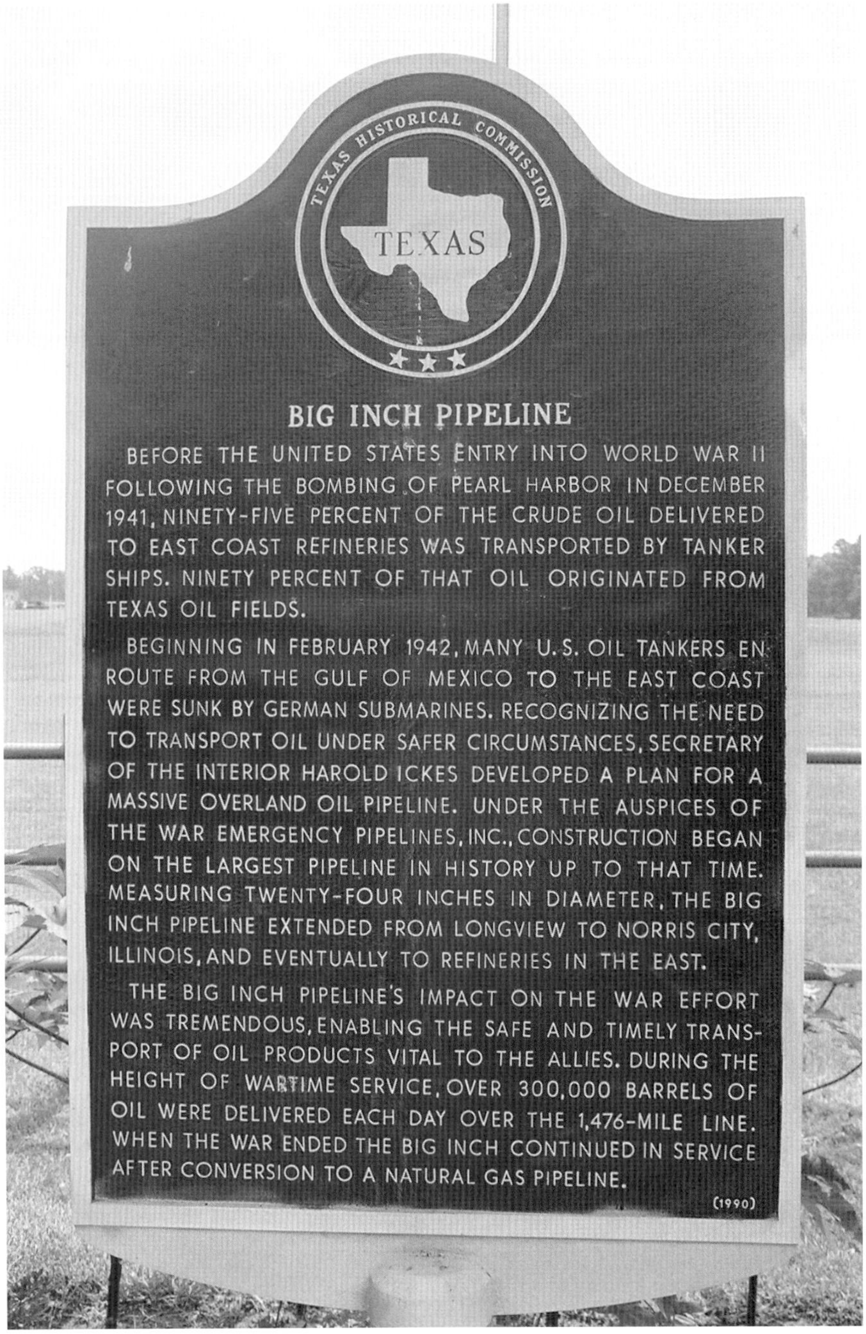

❖

The Big Inch pipeline ran 1,400 miles from Gregg County to East Coast refineries. Built during World War II, more than 262 million barrels of oil had flowed through the largest crude-oil pipeline ever laid. It's said Allied troops in Europe "rode to victory on East Texas crude" during the war.

COURTESY OF THE GREGG COUNTY HISTORICAL MUSEUM.

AN ENGINEERING MARVEL

The East Texas Oil Field, which made Gregg County rich beyond imagination, helped the Allies ride to victory in Europe.

The reason was one of the world's engineering marvels—the Big Inch pipeline that originated at Longview and traveled more than 1,400 miles to the major East Coast refineries. A whopping 24 inches in diameter, the Big Inch was the largest crude-oil pipeline ever laid. It took 15,000 workers to make it reality.

At the start of the war, East Texas remained the world's largest oil field. But the problem was getting that ocean of oil to the refineries back East and ultimately to our fighting troops overseas. German submarines operating along the Atlantic Coast were sinking oil tankers. Transportation of petroleum from the Gulf Coast to the East Coast had dropped from well over 1 million barrels daily to only 70,000 barrels.

A year or so before the Japanese attack on Pearl Harbor, U.S. Interior Secretary Harold Ickes had convinced President Franklin Roosevelt that an overland crude-oil pipeline from East Texas to the East Coast would be vital to any war effort. So in August 1942 the huge project began. The line would be owned by the federal government but built through a private firm, War Emergency Pipelines Inc.

The 24-inch pipe was made in 40-foot lengths with each length weighing some two tons. The first section of the Big Inch was to run 531 miles from Longview through Little Rock, Arkansas, across the Mississippi River to Norris City, Illinois That section of the line was completed February 20, 1943. From Illinois the line then extended to Phoenixville, Pennsylvania, and Linden, New Jersey. Experts said the project would take two years. It was accomplished in only half that time.

Thanks to the Big Inch, and later to a smaller 20-inch pipeline, more than 300,000 barrels of crude oil and refined products were being delivered daily to the Eastern Seaboard. The trip from Gregg County to the New York area took fourteen days. Soon, American and Allied tanks and jeeps in Europe were running on East Texas crude. By the end of the war, more than 262 million barrels of oil had flowed through the Big Inch.

Secretary Ickes called the pipeline "a triumph of teamwork unsurpassed" and "ingenious engineering." The Big Inch truly was an unsung hero of World War II. One wartime publication noted that the Big Inch was "more than a metal conduit for moving oil; it is a symbol of American spirit, an expression of a determined people whose purpose is freedom."

Following the war, the Big Inch was converted to a natural-gas pipeline operated by Texas Eastern Transmission Corporation.

In November 1945 Gregg County lost one of its most popular public servants with the death of Dush Shaw, who had been county clerk for almost fifty years.

"THE LORD HAD SOMETHING IN MIND"

The day of February 1, 1946, was an important one in Gregg County. That's when title to the former Harmon General Hospital was officially transferred to Mr. and Mrs. R. G. LeTourneau. That sealed the LeTourneaus' decision to locate a giant manufacturing plant at Longview and paved the way for what today is LeTourneau University.

Harmon General Hospital, which had served the U.S. military during World War II, counted 220 buildings on its 160 acres. A total twenty-five thousand wartime patients came through its doors between December 1942 and December 1945.

It wasn't long after that before efforts were under way to transfer title to the property to industrialist and inventor LeTourneau, who dreamed of establishing a college. It would be a school, he said, that would offer programs to returning war veterans who could earn a living at LeTourneau's new plant while getting an education at the same time.

In his autobiography titled *Mover of Men and Mountains*, LeTourneau recalled, "I had gone out hunting for a plant site adjacent to a steel mill, but the Lord had something in mind. He wanted a school in which to train Christian engineers, and let me build my steel mill adjacent to it." The government liked the idea and transfer of ownership was prepared.

Carl L. Estes, publisher of the *Longview News-Journal*, spearheaded the drive to raise funds to purchase several thousand acres to locate the manufacturing plant. "We are to meet him dollar for dollar in the establishment of the LeTourneau Technical Institute of Texas," Estes wrote in a front-page editorial. "We—you and I, must show this great man that we believe in ourselves as much as he believes in us." On February 24 the school was dedicated before a large crowd.

Ever so slowly, the original wooden hospital barracks were replaced by impressive brick structures on campus. A modern residence hall was built in 1962. Then came the Margaret Estes Library, a science building, lab buildings, a gymnasium and engineering building. The 1970s and 1980s brought more dorms, the Longview Citizens Resource Center, the R.G. LeTourneau Memorial and Student Center, and other projects. In 2005 the college began its largest-ever construction project. The $20-million S. E. Belcher, Jr., Chapel and Performance Center seats 2,011 for concerts and productions.

LeTourneau's manufacturing plant, which produced heavy road and earth-moving machinery, obtained its needed iron and steel from Lone Star Steel Co. in Morris County.

The month of July 1946 saw a meeting of Gregg and Rusk County residents to discuss plans for a four-thousand-acre lake on Cherokee

Above: Located at 322 Teague Street in Longview, this is one of the few remaining structures of the early settlement of Earpville. The north boundary of the tract was on a stagecoach line that ran between Shreveport, Louisiana, and Tyler.

COURTESY OF THE GREGG COUNTY HISTORICAL MUSEUM.

Below: Originally called Hotel Longview, in 1934 Conrad Hilton bought the downtown business and doubled its capacity during the East Texas oil boom. The hotel was the scene of many an oil deal. Heritage Plaza now sits on the site.

COURTESY OF THE GREGG COUNTY HISTORICAL MUSEUM.

Bayou, located halfway between Longview and Henderson. Banker V. A. Clements was named general chairman of the project, which would require a dam to be constructed across the bayou.

"Completion of the project will provide excellent hunting, fishing and boating almost at the doorsteps of the citizens in this area and it is expected that summer homes and hunting and fishing lodges eventually will dot the eight-mile shoreline," said a contemporary newspaper report.

In 1948 a $592,105 bid was accepted by directors of the Cherokee Water Company for construction of the dam at Lake Cherokee. Earth work for the lake was handled by R.G. LeTourneau's huge earth-moving machinery.

By 1951, with construction of the lake and completion of a new filtration plant, the city of Longview began using Lake Cherokee as its major water-supply source. Prior to the discovery of oil in 1930-31, Longview used the Sabine River for its water supply. Later, water was obtained twenty-two miles away from Little Sandy Creek.

TEXAS EASTMAN BRINGS JOBS

In 1950, land began to be cleared for what would prove to be the area's largest employer. The 2,400-acre tract for Eastman Kodak Company's Texas operation was located south of Longview in Harrison County. "The transformation of a sleepy and dense forest region on the banks of the Sabine River to a busy industrial site is a chapter in the story of postwar development in East Texas," a contemporary newspaper article reported.

Texas Eastman Co. began operations in January 1952 to manufacture plastics and industrial chemicals. Growth and expansion of the company and its product lines made it an important supplier to firms in the chemicals and plastics industries. Eastman officials had selected the area due to availability of water, rail lines and needed raw materials. Texas Eastman became the area's largest employer with more than 2,000 employees.

❖

Right: R. G. LeTourneau opened a manufacturing plant and technical institute in Longview after World War II. Located on the former site of Harmon General Hospital, the school today is LeTourneau University.

COURTESY OF THE GREGG COUNTY HISTORICAL MUSEUM.

Other major projects of the time included completion of the four-story Bramlette Building in downtown Longview, an $800,000 expansion of Gregg Memorial Hospital, a new 50-bed general hospital in Kilgore costing $842,000, a new Texas and Pacific freight depot, several industrial plants and the $18-million Knox Lee Power Plant built by Southwestern Gas & Electric Company. In 1954 Lake Gladewater was built.

A modern Gregg County Airport was formally dedicated July 15, 1947, with Mid-Continent ready to provide four daily flights and Delta Airlines planning service which began in December that year. However, work on the 521-acre facility—later expanded to 800-plus acres—had begun as early as 1939.

Originally a Works Project Administration (WPA) project, ground was broken in April

Bottom, left: This aerial view shows the 220 Harmon General Hospital buildings that served LeTourneau Technical Institute students for many years. Today, LeTourneau University boasts modern facilities on its ever-expanding campus.

COURTESY OF THE GREGG COUNTY HISTORICAL MUSEUM.

Bottom, right: LeTourneau Technical Institute of Texas opened in 1946 on the site of the former Harmon General Hospital, closed by the military at the end of World War II.

COURTESY OF THE GREGG COUNTY HISTORICAL MUSEUM.

1941 for the $407,556 airport. County Judge Merritt H. Gibson, using a spade dropped from a plane, turned the first dirt on the project. According to a contemporary report, "Civic leaders of Kilgore and Gladewater joined with those of Longview in the ceremonies while the Army bombers from Barksdale Field flew overhead."

Immediately after the groundbreaking, W. K. Woodruff, regional WPA engineer, ordered a crew of 100 to begin clearing the site. Eventually 750 workers were involved in the airport's construction.

In 1950 a Gregg Countian, John Ben Shepperd, was appointed Texas secretary of state at the age of thirty-four. Born October 19, 1915, in Gladewater, Shepperd graduated from the University of Texas at Austin, became a lawyer and served as a Gregg County commissioner. Shepperd was Jaycees' national president in 1947-48 and the following year was named one of the country's "Ten Outstanding Young Men." (Also honored that year was a young man from Michigan named Gerald Ford.)

Shepperd served on the State Board of Education and in 1952 was elected state attorney general. Two years later he won re-election to the statewide post. He was a leader in the Democratic Party for many years and served as a political adviser to President Lyndon B. Johnson. Involved in education, historical preservation, business and cultural organizations, Shepperd in 1984 was named "Texan of the Year" by the Texas Chambers of Commerce. Shepperd died in March 1990 at the age of seventy-four.

The county's first commercial television station aired in 1951. KTVE, Channel 32, an ultra-high frequency (UHF) station owned by A. James Henry, was located in a small studio midway between Longview and Kilgore. The station was in operation for five years before going off the air in 1955. "We broadcast from about 1:30 in the afternoon until about 10:30 at night," recalled Henry in an interview years later. "But that's a long time to have to fill up when you don't have a network affiliation … You had to buy a special converter and put up a special antenna to receive our (UHF) signal."

Lawrence "Sonny" Birdsong was the station's music director who played the organ and piano. A musical show featured Tubby Wallace and the Honey-Drippers. Other local programming included a cooking show, square-dancing, public school academic competitions and a children's show hosted by Wesley Dean as "Ranger Wes."

The Joseph B. Bramlette Building in Longview was one of many such downtown office structures built in the county during the 1940s and 1950s.

COURTESY OF THE GREGG COUNTY HISTORICAL MUSEUM.

A TEXAN CONQUERS THE SOVIET UNION

In 1956 the county got its first "skyscraper," the 10-story First National Bank in downtown Longview. Original plans called for a 16-story structure—which at the time would have been one story higher than Tyler's tallest office building. But the Longview project eventually was scaled back. Through the years several banks have called it home, most recently Chase Bank.

Gregg County residents proudly celebrated the triumph of Kilgore's own Van Cliburn, who in 1958 won the coveted Tchaikovsky International Piano Competition in Moscow—at the age of twenty-three. Harvey Lavan Cliburn Jr. was born in Louisiana. His parents moved to Kilgore when he was six years old. By age twelve he had won a statewide piano competition that allowed him to debut with the Houston Symphony. At age seventeen he entered The Julliard School of Music.

After winning the Tchaikovsky competition, the affable Cliburn received a ticker-tape parade in New York City and became the world's most popular pianist. He had the first classical album to sell a million copies. In 1962 he became artistic adviser for the prestigious Van Cliburn International Piano Competition in Fort Worth.

Longview experienced its largest annexation in fifty-five years when, on December 31, 1959, the city took in the community of Greggton. Several thousand people were added to Longview's population count and paved the way for the city's continued expansion to the north and west.

The decade of the 1950s turned out to be one of rapid growth and expansion for Gregg County. Numerous nationally known industries established operations in the county, including ITT Bell & Gossett Company, Resistol Hat, Screw & Bolt Corporation of America. By mid-decade business and civic leaders formed a non-profit corporation, Longview Industrial Districts Inc.—headed by industrialist Robert Cargill—to purchase additional land for development.

The county population by 1960 grew to 69,436 (Longview was 40,050; Kilgore 10,092; and Gladewater 5,742).

❖

Right: Kilgore's Van Cliburn won the coveted Tchaikovsky International Piano Competition in Moscow at the age of twenty-three. He became the first musician to receive a ticker-tape parade in New York City.

COURTESY OF KILGORE COLLEGE.

Below: Gladewater's business district was abuzz with activity during oil-boom days. Today, Gladwater is known as the "Antique Capital of East Texas."

COURTESY OF THE GREGG COUNTY HISTORICAL MUSEUM.

Chapter VIII

An Interstate, Beer & Diversification

Construction on Loop 281 around north Longview started in 1964 and Interstate 20 came through Gregg County two years later. During the decade a major beer brewery, operated by Schlitz (Stroh), built in Longview.

In 1966, Gregg County had the distinction of hosting the first "Beatles Bonfire" west of the Mississippi River, all because of a remark made by John Lennon. He'd said, "We're more popular than Jesus now." Lennon later said he meant it was strange that young people should be more concerned with rock music than religion, but the damage was done. Soon some Americans were boycotting the Beatles' music. Longview station KLUE called for records, photos and other Beatles paraphernalia to be collected for a huge bonfire. On the night of August 12—a day after the Beatles left England for their first U.S. tour—thousands gathered for the local bonfire. Within minutes a heaping mound of Beatlemania was turned to ashes. That should have been the end of the story, but the very next day something strange happened. A bolt of lightning struck KLUE's transmission tower, rendering deejay Phil Ransom unconscious and knocking the station off the air. Coincidence? Probably. But local diehard Beatles fans were hard to convince.

In 1970 a ten-thousand-foot runway was completed at Gregg County Airport, making it the first civilian airport in the Southwest to offer a runway that long. A new traffic-control tower was built in 1976 and the terminal building was renovated and expanded in 1987-88.

In 1972 the City of Longview opened a most unusual park—a narrow 2.2-mile trail that formerly had been a failed railroad line. Cargill Long Park, a National Recreation Trail, had been part of the line for the Port Bolivar and Iron Ore Railroad that ran from Ore City, Upshur County, through Longview to the Gulf Coast. Robert Cargill, Sr., bought the line in 1953. Two decades later he and wife Pauline gave the railroad right of way to the city.

❖

Lake Cherokee, completed in the early 1950s, serves as a local water supply and provides recreational opportunities for residents living on the shores of the four-thousand-acre lake on Cherokee Bayou.

COURTESY OF THE GREGG COUNTY HISTORICAL MUSEUM.

The trail, whose master plan called for a nine-mile route, quickly became popular with residents for its pine-shaded path, flower gardens, picnic areas and playgrounds.

THE BALLOON CAPITAL OF TEXAS

Area residents had a major new place to shop when the seven-hundred-thousand-square-foot Longview Mall, a regional shopping center, opened with much fanfare in 1978. That same year the Great Texas Balloon Race began at the mall. The unique event, now featuring eighty-plus professional hot-air balloonists, since has relocated to East Texas Regional Airport (formerly Gregg County Airport) and earned Longview the title "Hot-Air Balloon Capital of Texas."

The year 1980 saw the opening of what now is called Longview Regional Medical Center. Through the years several expansions have taken place at the 166-bed hospital, including a $14-million, 100,000-square-foot medical office building in 2004.

Right: Robert "Bob" Cargill Sr. headed Longview Industrial Districts Inc. He and wife Pauline gave railroad right-of-way to the city of Longview for development of Cargill Long Park, a National Recreation Trail.

COURTESY OF THE GREGG COUNTY HISTORICAL MUSEUM.

One of Gregg County's top tourist attractions opened in 1980. The unique East Texas Oil Museum, on the campus of Kilgore College, was funded by Placid Oil Company and the family of famed Texas oilman H. L. Hunt. The twenty-thousand-square-foot structure—complete with a huge oil derrick out front—contains major exhibits, photographs, antique autos, tools and other artifacts from oil-boom days, including the re-creation of a 1930s' "Boomtown" street.

The "oil bust" of the early 1980s brought higher unemployment to the area. Depletion of oil resources and encroachment of salt water into the field also affected Gregg County's economy. Business and population growth slowed but local officials learned the importance of diversification.

Below: The ten-story First National Bank building in downtown Longview was built in the mid-1950s. Today it is home to Chase Bank.

COURTESY OF THE GREGG COUNTY HISTORICAL MUSEUM.

Bottom, right: The Great Texas Balloon Race, held at East Texas Regional Airport, annually attracts many of the nation's top professional hot-air balloonists.

COURTESY OF THE GREGG COUNTY HISTORICAL MUSEUM.

During the decade Gladewater became one of the first cities in East Texas to offer businesses tax-abatement incentives, attractive to firms wanting to relocate because they receive tax breaks. A number of antique shops and specialty shops were attracted downtown, earning Gladewater the title "Antique Capital of East Texas."

In 1984 Maude Cobb Convention and Activity Center, a forty-thousand-square-foot facility, opened in Longview. It replaced a smaller exhibit building at the Gregg County Fairgrounds—later purchased from the Jaycees by the city and renamed Longview Fairgrounds—as the county's largest meeting facility.

A special city park serving disabled children opened in Longview in February 1984. Rotary Park, funded by local Rotarians and 90 other organizations, features a specially designed merry-go-round, swing set, spray pool, and restrooms.

In 1984 the county's first commercial television station since 1955 went on the air. KLMG, Channel 51, was a CBS affiliate. It later changed its call letters to KFXK and became a Fox affiliate.

The city of Longview opened a new public library building in 1986 and the *Longview News-Journal* moved into a new 60,000-square-foot, three-story structure in 1988. Good Shepherd Medical Center opened its Heart Center in 1987, following with a $15-million care unit and a five-story, 105,000-square-foot Medical Plaza office building.

The decade of the 1980s also saw Longview's largest annexation since 1959 with annexation of the area comprising the Spring Hill Independent School District.

Gregg County lost one its most popular and recognizable residents in 1991 with the death of Hubert Gregg, ninety-two. Known for decades as the "Peanut Man," Gregg moved to the county in 1931 and the following year began selling peanuts. For many years the blind peanut vendor traveled Longview's streets with his guide dog, walking stick and a red wagon filled with goobers. He was a regular at local sporting events, too. In 1993 a plaque was dedicated in his memory at Longview Independent School District's Lobo Stadium—at the very spot where Gregg had sold his peanuts on Friday nights.

A Race Relations Committee was organized in 1995 by the City of Longview's Partners in Prevention to provide "a forum for dialogue critical to achieving the goal of equal opportunity and fair treatment for all members of society." The organization's statement of purpose includes these words: "The Committee recognizes that harmonious race relations are not achieved by any one act, but are a journey of growth requiring continuing self-examination and change."

By the 2000 census Gregg County had 111,379 residents. City populations included Longview, 73,344; Kilgore, 11,301; Gladewater, 6,078; White Oak, 5,624; and Liberty City, 1,935.

A BRIGHT FUTURE INDEED

The face of Gregg County has changed dramatically since the oil-boom days.

15

Above: Northside Elementary School faculty, 1961, included (back, from left) Mrs. W. Griffin, Mrs. Sidney Willis, Mrs. G. E. Robinson, Mrs. Taylor, Mrs. R. E. Ellis, unidentified, Mrs. C. G. Garrett; (front, from left) G. Adams, Mrs. S. B. Murphy, Mrs. S. V. Jones, Jason W. Whitaker, unidentified, W. T. Willis.

COURTESY OF THE GREGG COUNTY HISTORICAL MUSEUM.

Below: The Mary C. Womack High School football squad, circa 1962. Following integration, a portion of the Womack High building housed the city of Longview's parks department.

COURTESY OF THE GREGG COUNTY HISTORICAL MUSEUM.

24

"Diversification" has been the key word in recent years as the East Texas Oil Field no longer dominates Gregg County's economy, which has rebounded from the oil bust of the 1980s. New commercial and retail projects are under way. In recent years local hospitals have seen major growth, increasing the region's importance as an acute-care medical center. Educational opportunities have expanded, too, with Kilgore College enlarging its Longview campus to meet student demand and the University of Texas at Tyler opening its Longview University Center in the fall of 2000.

Texas Eastman, now a part of Eastman Chemical Co., spent $35 million in 2004 on improvements to its hydrocarbon cracking plants. In 2005 a national publication ranked the Longview-Marshall metropolitan area, which includes Gregg County, as one of the best places in the U.S. for doing business.

Increasing numbers of retirees also have been drawn to the area's mild climate and leisurely lifestyle that features hunting, fishing, boating and other recreational activities.

With an abundance of water and other natural resources, a lower-than-average cost of living and a growing, healthy economy, Gregg County appears poised for continued growth in the twenty-first century.

But the East Texas Oil Field remains important. In October 2005 a "Diamonds and Silver" jubilee was held to celebrate the seventy-fifth anniversary of the field and the twenty-fifth anniversary of the East Texas Oil Museum at Kilgore College. Since discovery of oil in 1930, the field has produced more than 5 billion barrels of oil with an additional 1 billion barrels yet to be retrieved.

The story of Gregg County shows that history does indeed repeat itself. In 1957 the Longview Junior Chamber of Commerce published a pictorial history of Gregg County. In its introduction the book noted:

"The recollections show that Gregg County has a lusty heritage and has prospered in the face, at times, of adversity. (The county) has been able to rise to the occasion and meet the demands placed on its citizenry to keep pace with the state, the nation and the world."

Those words still ring true a half-century later.

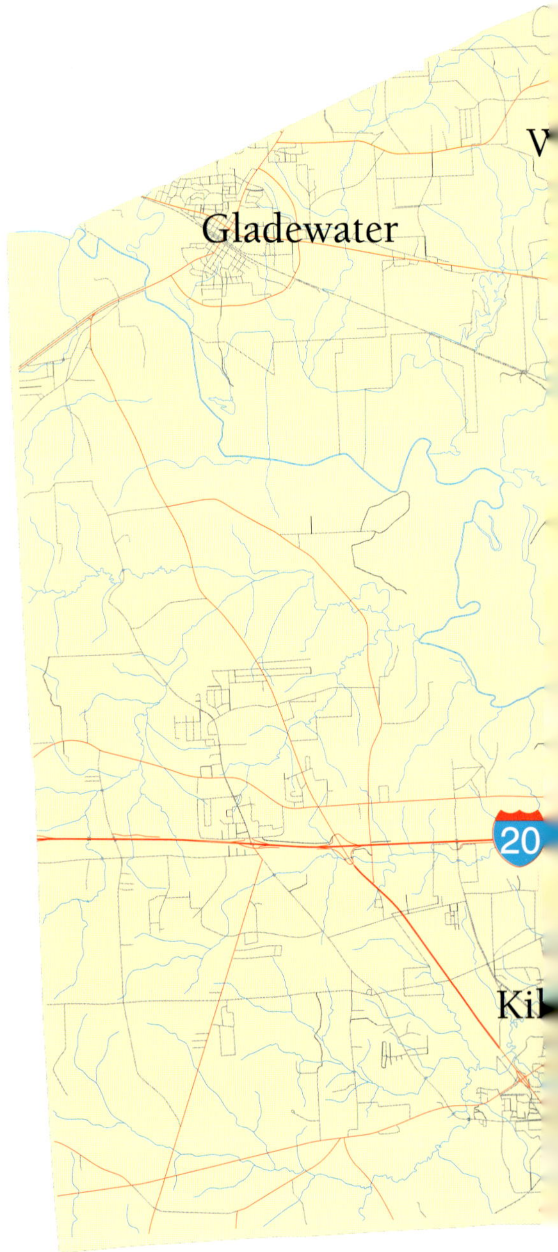

Gregg County, created in April 1873, was formed from portions of Upshur and Rusk counties by an act of the Thirteenth Texas Legislature. The county originally was to be called Roanoke County but instead was named in honor of General John Gregg. This map shows Gregg County as it appears today.

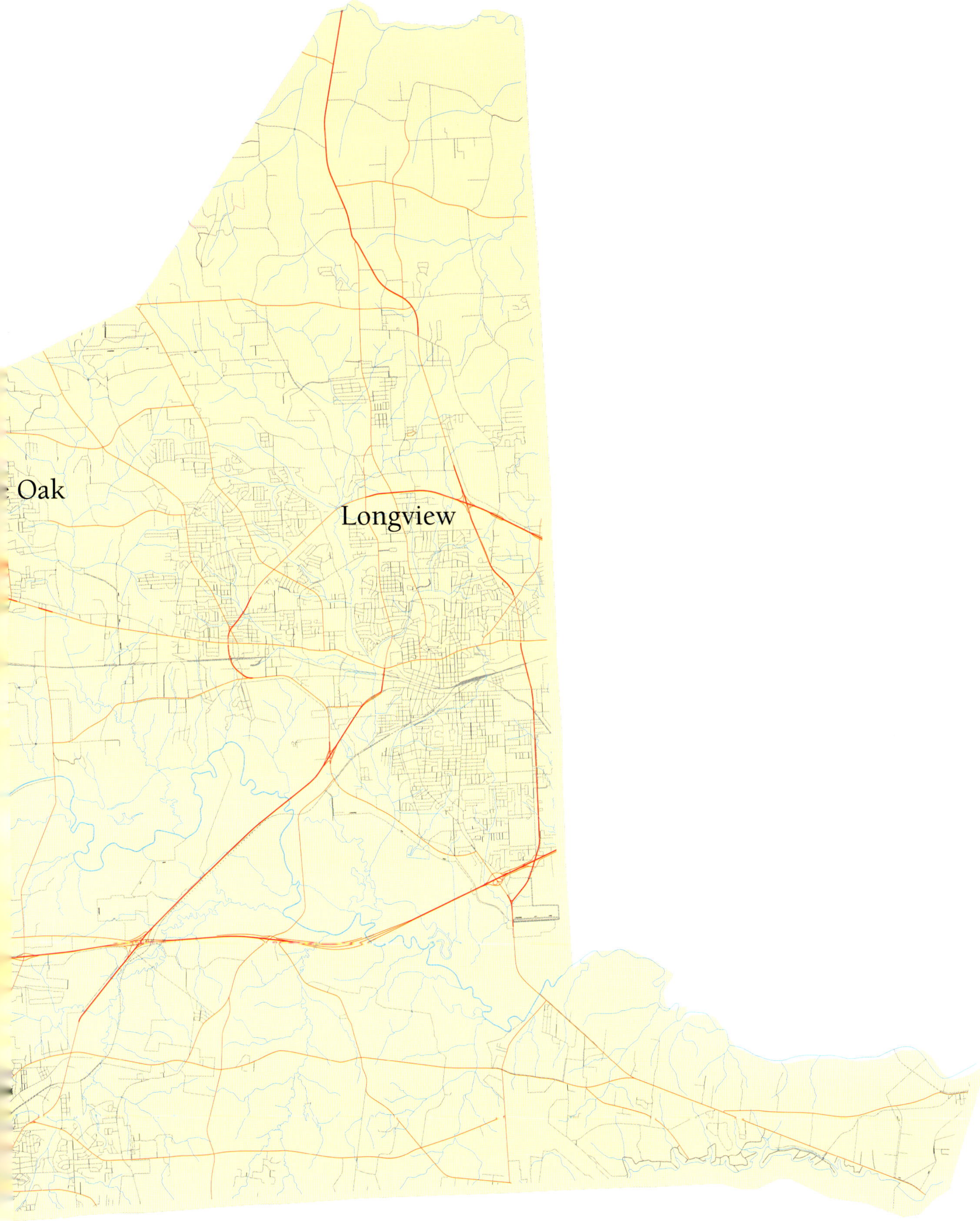
Oak
Longview

❖

A popular attraction at the East Texas Oil Museum, located on the Kilgore College campus, is "Boom Town," which recreates a muddy street scene during the height of the East Texas oil boom.

COURTESY OF KILGORE COLLEGE

❖

The Joe Anderson family shows off its crop of sweet potatoes. While cotton was a mainstay of the economy, farmers also grew corn, melons, peanuts, oats, sorghum, and other crops.

COURTESY OF THE GREGG COUNTY HISTORICAL MUSEUM

❖

Produce travels Longview's Tyler Street at the turn of the century. In the background is the First National Bank.

COURTESY OF THE GREGG COUNTY HISTORICAL MUSEUM

Sharing the Heritage

historic profiles of businesses, organizations, and families that have contributed to the development and economic base of Gregg County

Special Thanks to

McKenzie Transportation

Eastman Chemical Company

The East Texas landscape was changed, both literally and figuratively, when Tennessee Eastman Corporation announced that the Longview area had been chosen as the site for a new plant.

The Longview Daily News and the Marshall News Messenger trumpeted the news in the only edition the two papers ever published together. The banner headline on the August 25, 1949, afternoon edition proclaimed "Gregg-Harrison Counties Selected for Big Plant."

The front page included an aerial photo of the Kingsport, Tennessee plant, where the company was and still is headquartered, showing a plant that seemed to stretch as far as the eye could see. A Western Union telegram from the company president thanked the community for its support in helping the company reach its decision.

"We trust that the relations between our company and the citizens of your community will always be pleasant and mutually advantageous," wrote James C. White, president of Tennessee Eastman Corporation.

White turned out to be somewhat of a prophet. The community welcomed the company with open arms, and throughout the intervening years the company has thanked the community by providing jobs to East Texas residents, paying millions in taxes, purchasing goods and services from East Texas companies to further stimulate the economy, and by providing many leaders for local nonprofits, schools, and government needs.

The plant began as a satellite facility to supply materials to the home plant in Tennessee or to Eastman Kodak Company in Rochester, New York. East Texas ingenuity and talent merged with expertise imported from other Eastman facilities to create an environment of innovation and creativity. The people who came to the Longview facility were scientists, engineers, managers, and East Texas farm hands and oil field workers with their good work ethic; all blended well to develop a can-do attitude with a creative bent.

Texas Eastman Division, as it was later named, developed its own research and development capabilities, learned how to make specialty plastics, and built a lab and technical service capability that allowed it to become a full-service player in the chemical business.

The Longview plant is one of several Eastman Chemical Company manufacturing sites. The company employs approximately 15,000 people in more than 30 countries. Founded in 1920 to supply basic photographic chemicals to Kodak, Eastman Chemical Company became an independent, publicly traded company in January 1994. Sales revenue for 2003 was $5.8 billion.

Eastman is the largest producer of polyester plastics for packaging in the world and is a leading supplier of raw materials for paints and coatings, inks and graphic arts, adhesives, textile sizes, other formulated products, and cellulose acetate fibers.

EASTMAN LOCATES HERE
The Longview Daily News — COMBINED EDITION
MARSHALL NEWS MESSENGER — COMBINED EDITION
Gregg-Harrison Counties Selected For Big Plant
This Is Parent Plant of Tennessee Eastman Corporation At Kingsport
WESTERN UNION
Plant Site North Of Sabine River
Marshall Publisher Lauds Estes As "Dominant Force" Back Of Eastman Project
..An Appreciation
Texas Humor Spices Clark Inauguration
Tennessee Eastman Heads Express Thanks To Estes

Above: The only joint edition of the Longview News *and* Marshall News Messenger *in the history of both newspapers, announcing Eastman's decision to locate in Harrison County, Texas.*

Below: The first tank car of product shipped from the Longview facility in 1952.

❖

Above: Polyethylene blown film being observed and tested in the Plastics Laboratory.

Top, left: Aerial view of Eastman's Longview plant in 1960.

Below: View of the Hydrocarbon Cracking Plant 4.

All that means very little to anyone who isn't a chemist, but the products Eastman makes touch the lives of people around the world every day. In fact, Eastman manufactures and markets more than 1,200 chemicals, fibers, and plastic products.

Eastman's Longview facility is a major contributor to the company's success. Most of the plant is located in Harrison County, with a small part in Gregg County; but many of its employees hail from Longview as well as Marshall and many surrounding areas in Northeast Texas.

Today, the company receives and processes approximately 2.5 million gallons a day of feedstock–mostly propane and ethane delivered via pipeline–that go into making chemicals used as raw materials for a wide range of products. The facility, carved out of the wooded river bottom area of the Sabine River, covers 6,000 acres and the buildings and equipment where all the work is done cover 750 acres, a dramatic increase from the 100 acres utilized when the plant first opened. The company also operates a salt dome storage facility near Tyler that includes eleven underground storage wells having the capacity to safely store raw materials and chemical intermediates used at the plant.

Construction on the Longview plant began in 1950 and by March 1952 it shipped its first pound of product. Employment, which had begun with two people, soon reached 424. By 1957 the company added a second hydrocarbon cracking plant to process additional feedstock.

Other major events included the 1962 construction of a 250-mile-long pipeline from the Gulf Coast area south of Houston to Tyler. Two years later the company acquired an underground salt dome storage facility on a 330-acre site in Tyler.

Year after year the company expanded operations, adding buildings, operating units, and employees. It would take several pages to list all the changes that have occurred through the years. Two that can't be ignored are the $310 million hydrocarbon cracking plant and polyethylene expansion in 1983, and the $300 million expansion program that occurred in 1989.

Through the years, the company has been recognized for its safety and environmental record. In 1992, for instance, it was one of six businesses to receive the Environmental Protection Agency Administrator's Award for pollution prevention.

A year later it received the Texas Water Commission's Clean Industries 2000 Award for environmental excellence, and in 1994 received not only the prestigious Texas Quality Award but it was also named a STAR site under OSHA's

❖

Top, left: Maintenance personnel guiding heavy machinery.

Top, right: Eastman employees researching, developing, and testing new products.

Voluntary Protection Program. Eastman Chemical Company is also the only chemical company to ever win the Malcolm Baldrige National Quality Award.

The Longview plant, with approximately 1,800 employees, is one of the largest chemical plants owned by a single company in Texas. It manufactures more than sixty major chemical and plastic products sold to customers worldwide and in 2003 shipped 3.4 billion pounds of product, or 9.3 million pounds each day.

A very recent development is the purchase of a state-of-the-art electricity generating plant that produces 440 MW of electricity. Approximately 200 MW of power are supplied onto the local electricity grid. That is more than enough to power the City of Longview.

It owns and operates eight pipelines, three of which run 200 miles to the Gulf Coast. The facility has its own environmental staff of fifteen and has spent more than $500 million on environmental operating, development, and capital projects since 1981.

Noted economist Ray Perryman estimates that the direct, indirect, and induced impact of Eastman's Texas operations accounts for twenty percent of the total economy for the Longview-Marshall region.

In 2001, company expenditures in East Texas were over $280 million. Eastman personnel employed in the Longview area received more than $122 million in pay and benefits and the company paid more than $14.5 million in state taxes alone. All that economic activity resulted in more than 21,000 full-time equivalent jobs in East Texas.

Beyond the economic benefits the company contributes is its commitment to making life better for people around the world through its innovative products and services, and by making continuous progress toward the vision of no accidents, injuries, or harm to the environment and to a commitment to report its global health, safety, and environmental performance. Eastman also pledges to lead its operations in ethical ways that increasingly benefit society, the economy, and the environment.

The company also contributes to the local community and the state. Eastman employees lead the way each year during the annual United Way fund drive, contributing about a fourth of the more than $1 million raised by United Way drives in the local area, which support over twenty community programs.

In 2002 the company received the Texas Partners in Education State Recognition Award for its leadership in developing innovative partnerships with schools. The company's Nature and Wildlife Habitat Program, which provides the local schools an opportunity for science and biology studies outside the classroom, was a key factor in winning this award.

Eastman Chemical Company has a long-standing history of supporting and participating in efforts that enhance the quality of life where its employees live and work, and the company is committed to continuing that tradition while striving for excellence in everything it does.

Longview Partnership

The Longview Partnership is more than just a catchy name. It is a reflection of the community's willingness to work together to make Longview and the surrounding area a better place to live and work.

The Partnership, which is the city's chamber of commerce, came into existence in 1994 when the Longview Chamber of Commerce, the Longview Downtown Development Corporation, and the Longview Convention and Visitors Bureau merged.

The Greater Longview Organization for Business and Education (a state-recognized program to boost students' high school achievement) and 100 Acres of Heritage (dedicated to preserving Longview's central business district) became a part of the partnership umbrella in subsequent years.

The Partnership's primary mission is to enhance economic growth by focusing on education, promotion, and developing the business community. It offers its eleven-hundred-member constituency an array of opportunities through which they can help their community.

Governmental affairs, economic development, education, leadership development, and small business development are among the areas in which the Longview Partnership takes a leadership role and provides members with opportunities to serve.

Its influence is evident in the region's economic growth, as Longview's standard economic indicators have consistently shown positive trends in the past few years. In addition, major renovations in downtown Longview were a result, in part, to the Partnership's perseverance.

Tyler Street renovations, the development of Heritage Plaza, and KIDSVIEW, the state-of-the-art playground, owe much of their existence to the Partnership's efforts. The Partnership also sponsors the annual East Texas Boat, RV and Camping Exposition, ParBusters Scholarship Golf Tournament, the annual Business ShowCase, and the East Texas Economic Overview.

The Longview Convention and Visitors Bureau promotes Longview as a leisure destination and regional hub for tourism and small meetings, and helps local organizations solicit, plan, and host meetings, conventions, and special events.

The Partnership has been recognized as much as any Texas chamber of commerce through various competitions. The Partnership has won numerous awards for its economic development, community development, and education efforts.

The Longview Partnership is made up of people who want their community to grow and prosper and for their business to share in that prosperity. Working in conjunction with the Longview community, the Partnership plans to continue doing whatever it takes to enhance Longview's quality of life and create economic opportunities for everyone.

For more information on Longview or the Longview Partnership, please call 903-237-4000 or visit www.longviewtx.com.

❖

Below: Outdoor enthusiasts make it a point to attend the Longview Partnership's annual East Texas Boat, RV, and Camping Exposition each January.

Bottom: Businesses doing business with each other is the goal of the Longview Partnership's annual Business ShowCase each April.

LONGVIEW REGIONAL MEDICAL CENTER

For more than a quarter of a century, Longview Regional Medical Center has been leading the way in healthcare for the citizens of Longview and surrounding communities. Advanced technology, expanded services, a diverse staff and continued enhancements set the foundation for unprecedented growth and prosperity. The vision and dreams of Longview business and civic leaders and the foresight of the founders of Longview Regional are combined in the forces that helped open the doors for Longview Regional Medical Center in June 1980.

As a Level III Trauma Center, Longview Regional is reinforcing and strengthening the vision of the past in preparation for the potential it can achieve in the future. The medical center's tradition of caring, quality service and commitment to the community provides the momentum to seek new and better ways to provide proactive, cost-efficient healthcare for individuals and families throughout its expanding service area.

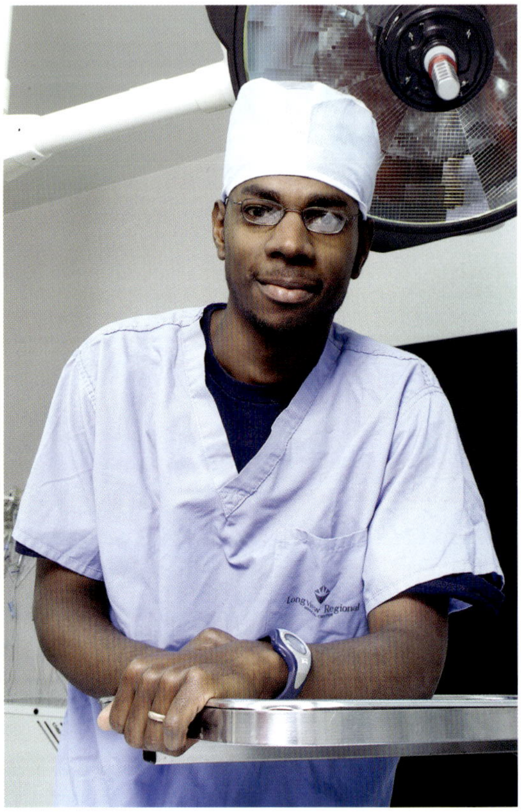

Over the past several years, Longview Regional has reached many milestones in caring for the community. In 2004 a record number of births for the newest additions to our community were recorded at Longview Regional Medical Center. The hospital also recently began Longview's only bariatric surgery program for the morbidly obese in response to the national epidemic of obesity.

Longview Regional Medical Center is also proud of achieving its exemplary patient, physician and employee satisfaction and to ensure this, they track satisfaction scores using a national, unbiased rating agency. The growing medical center's goal is for all patients to be very satisfied with the service and care provided to them.

As an employer, Longview Regional believes that being invested in the professional needs of its employees yields dividends in satisfied patients. The staff is passionate about the care that is provided at Longview Regional and the hospital cares about its employees. It is truly rewarding to know that both groups realize there is a difference at Longview Regional.

Longview Regional contributes to the community in many tangible and in other more difficult to quantify ways. In 2004 alone, the economic impact that Longview Regional had on our direct economy topped $41 million. Compound that staggering number by twenty-five years and one can begin to realize what the economic benefits to the community have been.

Many of the hospital's upper and middle management employees also participate in community service programs throughout the city. It is part of our "values" commitment as an organization.

Many may not be aware that Longview Regional Medical Center has the only local Physician Leadership Group (PLG) and

Nursing Leadership Group (NLG) made up of local physicians and staff nurses whose singular focus is to address issues and create innovative ways to improve the health status of our community.

The hospital also offers the area's only employer relations program, which joins efforts with local employers to identify, address and eliminate employee health risks before they result in costly healthcare claims.

In addition, Longview Regional offers Longview's only hospital-based Skilled Nursing Care Facility, which provides services to patients after a three-night stay in an acute hospital. Patients requiring more central nursing and therapy can be admitted to this specialized unit to receive needed care. This is a unit where the care is provided by a multi-disciplinary team approach. Nurses, physicians, physical therapists, occupational therapists, speech therapists, planned activities and social services focus on the unique needs of patients of all ages. Skilled services include monitoring treatment of an acute or exacerbation illness, IV therapy, wound healing, and physical, occupational or speech therapy.

The hospital is also proud to have the area's only mobile women's services unit, which includes mobile mammography and a mobile bone density screening unit making screening more convenient and accessible in order to better meet the needs of the women of East Texas.

Longview Regional Medical Center takes great pride in offering exceptional services and a choice in healthcare providers to the people of East Texas.

Longview Regional Medical Center is located at 2901 North Fourth Street in Longview, Texas and on the Internet at www.longviewregional.com.

Holiday Inn Express Hotel & Suites

The Holiday Inn Express Hotel & Suites combines an attractive facility, convenient location and outstanding management to create a comfortable, relaxing and affordable lodging experience for your family and business needs.

Located off Interstate 20 in Longview, Holiday Inn Express offers ninety rooms, fifteen suites, a fully equipped business center and a level of personal and business amenities not usually found in smaller, more affordable hotels. Visit us and you'll see why we were voted Best Hotel in East Texas for 2003.

Our fresh, attractive and newly constructed facility offers guest meeting facilities for fifty people, an outdoor swimming pool, exercise facility, complimentary breakfast bar, free parking, valet and guest laundry facilities, express check-in and check-out and an indoor corridor to ensure customer safety.

Step inside one of our spacious, well-appointed rooms and you'll feel right at home, whether you need a place to work or a comfortable spot to relax while on the road. Each room comes with a business desk with two telephones, two lines and a speaker phone, voice mail and data ports, iron/ironing board, hair dryer, coffeemaker, electronic locks and 27-inch remote-control televisions with cable. Other amenities include high-speed Internet access, valet service, AM/FM radio and alarm clock, voice mail and suites with microwave and refrigerator.

Our Presidential Suite features two bedrooms completely separate from the living area. It includes a large bathroom, televisions in both the living area and bedroom, two sleeper sofas in the living area and a dining area that seats up to four with microwave, refrigerator and sink.

You won't find a higher standard of service in the lodging industry than that offered by Holiday Inn Express and its owners, Lodging Host Hotel Corporation. Lodging Host Hotel Corporation is known for innovation and excellence and is the operating entity behind many Holiday Inn, Best Western, Comfort Suites and Ramada Inn hotels.

Our world-class management team has unrivaled experience when it comes to meeting the rigorous demands of our clients. Working as a team and involving our employees at all levels, we provide a complete and effective range of hotel/motel services to lending institutions, corporate investors and the private sector.

We offer a full scope of hotel services in operations, construction, marketing, accounting, property development and real estate. Our hands-on approach and unsurpassed efforts guarantee our customers will enjoy their stay and that owners and investors will enjoy excellent financial performance, quality and peace of mind.

Our participatory management style has earned Lodging Host an excellent reputation for turning properties around. We've also developed innovative programs like our First Choice Club and direct Choice Reservations. With an eye on the bottom line, our operating efficiency provides the basis for reaching cost-effective goals while maintaining the quality of service that ensures guest satisfaction and a high reputation.

Once you've arrived in our spacious, comfortable lobby you'll immediately feel welcome. All your personal and business needs will be met and are all are accessible through the interior corridors. Begin your day in our spacious, relaxing breakfast area and enjoy a complimentary breakfast bar with an assortment of pastries, cereals, fresh fruits, juices, coffee and more. Our Express Start Breakfast is a Holiday Inn Express Standard, featuring our award-winning cinnamon roll known nationwide.

Our ability and willingness to go beyond the usual is apparent in our facilities, services and the return we bring to our investors, even when dealing with complex and difficult financial situations. Through the years, we've successfully responded to the uncertainty and volatility in the U.S. economy and looked beyond the typical techniques to accomplish our financial objectives.

We're grateful to our guests for their support and pledge to continue working hard to set standards of service and performance that are second to none. Contact anyone on our hotel staff to learn how we can make your stay in the Longview area the best possible, and call on our management team to find out how we can increase your bottom line and manage your hotel with excellence.

You may visit us on the Internet at www.longview-hotel.com or visit us at 900 South Access Road in Longview, Texas.

Four-S Oil Company, Inc.

❖

Marvin A. Smith working in the fields.

Four-S Oil Company is the corporate descendent of the Marvin A. Smith Company, founded in 1938 by the company's namesake to remove paraffin from East Texas' flowing oil wells.

Marvin came to the oil field in 1935 working as an independent oil operator. He began his company with a single pickup truck and a shop-made wire-line unit. He had little competition because the work was labor intensive, specialized and had slim profit margins.

But as East Texas oil fields aged, this provided other opportunities for service for the oil and gas industry, including swab units, paraffin melting units, wire-line units and, eventually, complete work-over units. Beginning with a single service, the company's work eventually grew to complete and diversified well servicing and employed 100 people in 1993.

Through the years, the company grew from $12,000 in annual sales to $6 million.

Marvin had help in founding the company. His wife, Constance, was a full partner in the business, always supporting her husband's endeavors and often joining him in the oil fields around the wells he produced. Their sons worked weekends and summers while in high school, thus learning the oil service business.

Marvin and Constance ran the company until Denny graduated from North Texas State University and returned to help. Marvin and Denny insisted that Mickey, who had graduated from Stephen F. Austin University and was employed by the Federal Deposit Insurance Corporation, quit his job and come help because the opportunities to expand were promising. Mickey, in turn, called his brother-in-law, Claude Holland, who was working for Hughes Tool, and insisted he take early retirement and join them. The company operated with the five family members in charge until its sale to employees in 1993.

Among the many employees who gave much of their time and labor to the company was A. D. Carver, operations manager, who did whatever it took to keep the rigs operating and contributed greatly to the success of the service company.

It was during the time after Denny, Mickey and Claude joined the company that Four-S Oil Company came into existence. Through the years, additional companies have been formed—Smith Partners Ltd. and MSC Property Management Ltd.—to meet changing customer needs and corporate interests.

Today, the children of Marvin and Constance Smith continue to operate the remaining family businesses. Denny M. Smith serves as president of Four-S Oil Company; Mickey D. Smith serves as managing partner of Smith Partners, Ltd.; and Sanny Sue Smith Holland serves as managing partner of MSC Property Management, Ltd.

In 1980, the family became involved in the waste management business by leasing property owned by Four-S Oil Company. The site serves Gregg County and surrounding counties and has the capacity to continue serving those counties for the next three decades.

Family members have served on numerous boards of financial institutions, community and university boards, professional organizations, local committees and are involved in their churches.

Denny Smith served as Gregg County commissioner from 1978 to 1984. Mickey Smith served as Kilgore city commissioner from 1975 to 1981, as mayor of Kilgore from 1981 to 1987 and as Gregg County judge from 1995 to 2003.

As for the future, the family plans to continue operation of its oil and gas production, to develop commercial real estate and continue managing land and financial investments.

Above: Marvin A. Smith with the paraffin cutting knives he designed.

Below: Back row, left to right: Denny Smith, Sanny Sue Smith Holland, and Mickey Smith. Front row, left to right: Marvin Smith and Constance Smith

THE CROSBY GROUP

The Crosby Group, Inc., is the leading source for accessories used in the lifting and material handling industry, providing the highest levels of quality control available. Based in Tulsa, Oklahoma, and with facilities in Longview, The Crosby Group has grown through a creative program of product development and aggressive acquisitions of leading lines.

Quality is so much a part of the Crosby culture that the terms "Crosby Only" or "Crosby or Equal" are standard language in industry contracts involving rigging products. To achieve and maintain these high standards, the company has developed the Crosby Communication System designed to convey the positive aspects of Crosby to the marketplace. It has identified six segments of its business that, when viewed as one, differentiate Crosby in the marketplace. These six segments are manufacturing, research and development, complete product line, customer service, engineering, and risk management.

The Crosby Group has compiled the most highly recognized brand names in the industry. Each has stood for quality for many years, and their uncompromising commitment to quality has made them the number one choice for several generations of end users. These companies include:

- Crosby (formerly Crosby-Laughlin, founded in 1836), makers of shackles, hooks, turnbuckles, links, rings, eyebolts, and wire rope clips.
- Lebus (founded 1941), makers of load binders, snatch blocks and tail chains.
- McKissick (founded 1925), makers of crane blocks, snatch blocks, and construction blocks and sheaves.
- National (founded 1954), makers of "Cold-Tuff" swage sleeves, swage buttons, swaging machines and dies.
- Western (founded 1883), makers of snatch blocks, tackle blocks, marine blocks and manila rope blocks.
- Bullard (founded 1952), makers of Golden Gate Hooks for use with wire rope, chain and hoists.

Lebus Manufacturing of Longview became part of The Crosby Group in 1956. Lebus loadbinders, snatch blocks and tail chains were highly recognized names in the Texas oil fields, providing quality second to none. Through the years, all the forging work for The Crosby Group has been moved to Longview to make use of its larger facilities.

Today, Lebus continues to emphasize the production of quality products. As with all Crosby facilities, extensive quality control systems are in place throughout every stage. The modern Longview facility uses the latest technology to prepare the high volume of dies needed for the forge shop. It also performs the machining and assembly of many of the forgings, and the plant's heat-treating furnaces offer all the capabilities to normalize and quench and temper products. The Longview facility is ISO 9001 Certified and forges the load binders, shackles, hooks, turnbuckles, links, rings and other products available through the Crosby line.

Crosby Group products are made with the highest design factors in the industry. They are better able to withstand abusive field conditions because of the improved impact and fatigue characteristics designed into each item. Most Crosby products are heat treated, a practice that allows products to deform when overloading occurs. This provides a warning signal before ultimate failure and that can save money and lives.

Crosby engineers all its products to perform, applying a wide range of engineering expertise that has resulted in Crosby being considered the standard in the industry. Quality control is maintained through product identification coding on the majority of steel purchased by Crosby. This allows traceability to its respective date of production and material certification.

The Crosby Group's commitment to research and development has led to many "firsts" in the industry. These firsts began as far back in the 1880s with production of the first forged wire rope clip and has continued to the present day.

Customer service at The Crosby Group means more than having the product available when you need it. It also means having a full-time, knowledgeable district sales representative available and a well-trained and fully equipped Customer Service Department and having a broad product line offering, a strong worldwide network of authorized Crosby distributors, a top-notch technical support team and a management team dedicated to ensuring all these services run smoothly.

A technical support team is ready to answer any questions in regard to products or services. This can be provided through training seminars and on-site engineering applications. These services provide important benefits such as improved risk management.

The Crosby Group has always been concerned that its users be knowledgeable with the installation, use, inspection, and maintenance of its products. The company offers a formal product instruction and warning program that includes features such as instruction sheets attached to individual items, comprehensive literature and a video training program. It also offers a complete on-site training program that can be customized to fit your needs.

With its commitment to quality and service, it's easy to see why The Crosby Group is the industry leader, a position it is dedicated to maintaining in the twenty-first century.

TEXAS BANK AND TRUST

Texas Bank and Trust began operations on March 4, 1958, under the name First State Bank of Longview. Four years later, after receiving trust powers, the bank changed its name to Longview Bank and Trust.

❖

Above: The Main Bank at 300 East Whaley in Longview.

Below: For the bank's twenty-fifth anniversary, artist and sculptor Henry Wedemeyer prepared six bronze relief panels to cover the limestone base for the 20-foot-by-38-foot American flag that had become the bank's hallmark.

The bank's founders, made up of a group of business and civic leaders, pledged their unwavering support to the community and announced their commitment to offering the finest quality service in East Texas.

J. Clyde Tomlinson, Sr., who served as chairman, and Norman Taylor, who served as president, would be pleased to see how successful their philosophy has proven to be. Longview-area residents responded to the bank's sincere efforts by placing their trust in the bank and its employees.

Through the years, Texas Bank and Trust, a name adopted in 2003 to reflect the bank's expanded influence, has been a strong, stable and independent force in fueling business growth, meeting customer needs and enhancing the quality of life for East Texas residents.

Stability has been an important component in the bank's success. Some two dozen employees have been with the bank twenty years or more, including its chairman and chief executive officer, Rogers Pope, who joined the bank in August 1969.

He's quick to tell you that the bank has been blessed through the years with an exceptionally capable and conscientious staff committed to the progress and well being of the communities it serves.

The bank places high value on community service. Bank officers and staff serve on boards and work as volunteers for civic, social, educational, cultural, and healthcare organizations. Bank officers historically have held positions of leadership with the Longview Partnership and Greater Longview United Way.

The bank's commitment to the community is reflected in its symbol, representing its commitment to individuals, businesses and the communities it serves. This well-known symbol now sports a Texas star at its core. The star represents the bank's proud heritage of strength, stability and tradition. Texas Bank and Trust has an equally proud history, and as it nears a half century of service it renews its pledge to the people of Longview and East Texas to do its best to keep the community's vibrant spirit alive, well and on the grow.

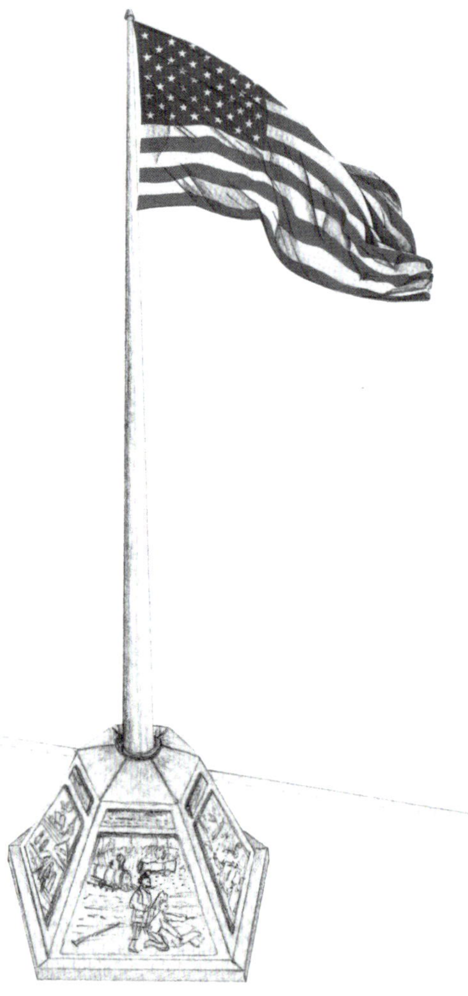

A&A Construction

The Adams family boasts a venerable history in the construction business, beginning more than eighty years ago with the founding of the Tom Adams Construction Company in Selma, Alabama. The business became a family affair several years later when son, Tom F. Adams, joined the firm.

In 1942, Tom F. Adams left the company for a stint with the Division 1866 combat engineers during World War II. Upon returning from the war, and after he completed his education at Morehouse College and Alabama College of Drafting and Architecture, Tom F. resumed working at his father's business, where he gained an apprenticeship in all facets of the construction business.

Tom F. Adams assumed management of the business after his father's death, continuing the legacy of the Tom Adams Construction Company for many years, as he managed the engineering, architecture, and on-site supervision of hundreds of construction projects.

He left Alabama in the 1960s, working for a while in Ohio, where he built several homes, and finally settling in Longview, Texas after marrying a local woman. In 1971, Adams formed a family corporation, A&A Construction, with his son Wayne Snoddy. Wayne is a graduate of the Ohio College of Applied Science, has a bachelor of science degree in mechanical engineering from Ohio University, and is a registered structural engineer in Texas, Louisiana, Oklahoma, Arkansas, Mississippi, and Ohio. Together, the two men have built a wide range of commercial, residential, and multi-family projects throughout the State of Texas.

In later years, A&A narrowed its focus to the construction of churches, and the firm has since built some of the most beautiful sanctuaries in the state. The year 1991 brought about the addition of A&A Design and A&A Reproduction, which are both owned and managed by Snoddy. These two subsidiaries handle the architectural and engineering work for many commercial and residential projects, while A&A Construction continues to be a leader in crafting fine houses of worship.

A&A Construction has built more than fifty churches over the years, in a variety of sizes and denominations. Local projects include the Red Oak Baptist Church, Harrison Street Church of Christ in Longview, the First Church of God in Christ in Killeen, College Hill Baptist Church and the East Texas Baptist Association Heritage Building in Tyler. A & A looks forward to carrying on the legacy of the Adams family, constructing sanctuaries and churches for many years to come.

❖

Below: Shiloh Baptist Church in Longview, Texas after renovations.

Bottom: Red Oak Baptist Church in Longview, Texas.

Coors of Longview

The relationship between Les Kroeger and Coors Brewing Company goes back much further than August 1975 when Coors chose Kroeger to own and operate its East Texas distributorship.

Kroeger grew up next to the Coors Brewery in Golden, Colorado and the site where his boyhood home once stood is now occupied by the company's third brewing vat. His dream of owning a Coors distributorship actually began in 1951 while drinking a beer with Adolph Coors II at the Coors Brewery workers' bar.

Kroeger, who worked part time for Coors for six summers while in school, thought it would be a great idea to own a distributorship and help the then-regional brand expand its market. But first he earned a bachelor's degree in business administration from the University of Northern Colorado, where he was selected outstanding wrestler in the Rocky Mountain Conference in 1957.

He then coached high school football and wrestling for two years before entering the business world. Kroeger worked ten years as a sales and marketing representative for the Adolph Coors Company and then spent three years as a sales manager for Ford Distributing Company. He also served as general manager for Coors Distributing of Fort Worth for five years before beating out a field of 300 applicants for the East Texas distributorship. Kroeger opened for business Thanksgiving week on November 24, 1975 and sold 17,000 cases of the already legendary brew.

Beginning with only thirteen employees, the company has expanded five times and now employs around sixty people. The business occupies 47,000 square feet of space, including 20,000 square feet of cold storage.

Coors of Longview is the wholesale distributor for Coors Brewing Company, Heineken, Pabst, Seagrams Coolers, Sam Adams, and Becks. Its marketing territory includes twelve counties in North East Texas. The company started with one brand and five packages and now has twenty-eight brands and 123 packages.

Much of the company's growth took place in 1995 when it purchased the local Stroh Beer Distributor, which increased the company's employee base from thirty-eight to fifty-six. Through the years, the company has grown to sell 1.5 million cases a year.

The future looks bright for Coors of Longview as it continues to build, grow and service its present market. The East Texas area can accommodate a large amount of population growth and the area's natural resources and strong workforce bodes well for East Texas and Coors of Longview.

MARTIN RESOURCE MANAGEMENT

Martin Resource Management of Kilgore is a leading independent provider of transportation, terminalling, marketing, and logistics management services for hydrocarbon products and by-products, chemicals, and other bulk liquids.

That's quite a statement when you consider its founder, R. S. Martin, Jr., started with a single truck and the simple desire to make a living for his family. Born in Camden, Arkansas, Martin graduated from Texarkana Arkansas High School in 1941 and attended the University of Arkansas until volunteering for the Marine Corps in February 1943. As a Marine, he served in the Fourth Marine division in four World War II invasions: Marshall Island, Saipan, Tinian, and Iwo Jima.

Returning to the University of Arkansas in 1946, he married Margaret Gerig of Arkadelphia, Arkansas, before graduating in 1948 with a business degree with a specialty in marketing. After two years with Continental Oil Company, he bought out his mother's and brother's interests in an ice company in Kilgore, Texas, with borrowed money.

In 1951, on borrowed money again, he started Martin Butane Company, driving the only truck while his wife kept the books and handled the billing. R. S. persevered with his dream of supplying fuel to drilling rigs in the East Texas oil field.

Today, the company owns more than $180 million in assets, consisting of a fleet of truck trailers, tank barges, pushboats/crewboats, bulk liquid terminalling locations, and other assets to serve its customers. Those customers include many Fortune 500 companies in industries such as petroleum, agriculture, petrochemical, and utilities.

Martin, a longtime Texan, couldn't possibly have foreseen the growth his small Martin Gas Corporation would experience. When he retired 35 years after buying that first truck, the company had grown to more than 1,000 employees and $500 million in sales. Martin died on September 20, 1999, leaving a legacy of entrepreneurship, hard work, and determination that remain Martin Resource Management hallmarks.

On November 6, 2002, Martin Resource Management sold a portion of its assets in a public offering. Martin Midstream Partners is a publicly held master limited partnership, listed as MMLP on the NASDAQ. The company R. S. Martin founded fifty years before is the general partner and majority owner. The founder's leadership and legacy is the company's guidance and will ensure Martin is the investment stockholders can depend on in the future.

❖

Martin Resource Management founder R. S. Martin, Jr.

Internal Medicine Association of Longview

The Internal Medicine Association of Longview has been a cornerstone of healthcare in East Texas since its inception in 1960. It began with one man's vision and determination to provide East Texans with improved healthcare services.

It all began in 1958 when Dr. John Vaughan opened a solo practice in leased space inside a downtown bank building. Two years later, Dr. Solon Coleman joined him and Internal Medicine Association of Longview was officially born.

In 1965, Dr. E. B. Edmondson joined the two original physicians and the three men built their own medical office building in partnership with another local physician. The building was located on Sixth Street near Good Shepherd Medical Center. Through the years, other physicians have joined the association and it has grown into a leading provider of primary care internal medicine in the East Texas area. The current members of IMA are Drs. Dan C. Jones, Kenneth M. Flory, Robert J. Sansom, Rodney B. Slone, Robert T. Tompkins, Lawrence H. Roe, C.R. Earnest, Srinivas Rangu, and Julia J. Archer. IMA's nurse practitioner is Melissa McNabb.

Internal Medicine Association is located on the first floor of Good Shepherd Medical Plaza II at 703 East Marshall Avenue. With approximately sixteen thousand square feet, the clinic offers complete adult primary care including laboratory services, diagnostic X-ray, pulmonary function testing, stress testing, EKGs and bone density analysis. IMA remains committed to providing the highest level of healthcare and wellness education. Guided by accurate diagnosis, open communication, individualized education, and state-of-the-art technology, IMA strives to improve the health and enrich the lives of its patients. In planning for the future, the association remains dedicated to meeting the healthcare needs of thousands of East Texans. Now, with nine internists, one nurse practitioner, and a support staff of forty-five, IMA is committed to maintaining the trust and confidence of its patients. IMA is proud to be part of such a diverse and dedicated medical community and thanks East Texans for allowing IMA the privilege of caring for them.

Above: Internal Medicine Association of Longview is located at 703 East Marshall Avenue.

Below: The members of the Internal Medicine Association of Longview (from left to right): Doctors Rick Earnest, Lawrence Roe, Kenneth Flory, Julia Archer, Dan Jones, Robert Sansom, Robert Tompkins, Rodney Slone and Srinivas Rangu.

Horaney's Inc.

Harry and Lorene Horaney opened their feed store in 1940 at 207 North Court Street in downtown Longview. It quickly became a favorite gathering place for people to visit, have a cup of coffee and buy feed for their livestock. They appreciated the warm, friendly atmosphere fostered by the Horaneys and knew they would either find what they needed or Harry and Lorene would go to any lengths to find it for them.

The store expanded and changed its merchandise through the years to keep up with customer demands. It added insecticides and chemicals followed by garden tools and garden equipment. Homeowners joined farmers as regular customers and Horaney's Feed Store flourished.

Harry and Lorene's son, Albert, joined the business after attending Texas A&M University. Albert had grown up in the store, joining his father after school and growing to appreciate both his father's business sense as well as his charitable ways.

In 1958, Albert married Betty Barkett of Marshall, and the two worked with Harry until his death in 1977. Albert decided that he needed a larger, more modern store, and in 1993 moved the business to its current location at 301 West Methvin Street.

Albert died in 1996, and in appreciation for his support for the Longview community the city changed the name of Court Street to Horaney Street. Betty continues to run the business with her son, Ron, while another son, Al, moved to Tyler to open a similar store.

Horaney's offers a wide range of products for its customers. They include farm supplies, feed, seed, pet supplies, hardware, bird supplies, cast iron, gift items and lawn supplies. Horaney's currently has ten employees and the store's reputation is known throughout East Texas.

The Horaney family has a long tradition of giving back to the community. Harry and Lorene started the tradition by helping out customers and fellow residents in need. The family has been involved with a wide range of charitable and community organizations through the years and will continue to do so.

The Horaneys look forward to continuing their support of the Longview and East Texas communities, and will make way for a fourth generation of family members—Betty's grandchildren—to join the family business.

You can visit Horaney's Inc. on the Internet at www.horaney.net.

All Seasons Window & Door Manufacturing, Inc.

Bill Akins founded All Seasons Window & Door Manufacturing, Inc. in 1979 in two rooms of a school gymnasium in the Fredonia community of Gregg County with five employees.

After building a new thirty-three-thousand-square-foot building in 1983 in Longview's Southwest Industrial Park, the company expanded its product line of storm windows and replacement windows and increased employment to twenty. By 1985 an additional product line of prime residential windows was added. Bill also began producing a premium line of insulated glass for his window lines. In 1989 the company increased its window line again to include heavy commercial hotel windows, and the following year added entry doors. A major expansion in 1993 increased the building to fifty-five thousand square feet for manufacturing and office space and included one of the South's largest window and door showrooms.

In 1999, Bill expanded the business by purchasing a heavy commercial window manufacturing company in Bryan, becoming a national and international supplier of quality windows. The Longview plant was already supplying windows to East Texas and Northwestern Louisiana and heavy commercial hotel windows to about twenty other states. The All Seasons Commercial Division added fifteen products and included customers all over the United States, Mexico, and military bases all over the world.

Another opportunity to expand fell into Bill's lap in 2000 when he purchased a local door manufacturing plant and added interior doors to the product line, making the company a one-source supplier for all window and door needs. Expansions of both the Longview and Bryan plants in 2001 made room to move the hotel window line to Bryan to produce all heavy commercial windows in that plant and to add the vinyl window line to the Longview location. The Longview plant now incorporates 104,000 square feet of manufacturing and office space.

The company has seen many changes in its twenty-five year history. The vinyl window line incorporates the latest state-of-the-art machinery used in the window industry. Continuous research and testing has resulted in new low-sound transmission products that are popular around airports and other high-noise areas. The fastest-growing product line is a now blast-resistant window sold to military installations.

Combining three great business endeavors—the design engineering of the windows, the architectural application of the variety of building products and the business management realm—has given Bill this unique opportunity. The Akins family is committed to its employees, customers and the Longview and Gregg County communities and the company is committed to high-quality products for its consumers.

All Seasons is located at 400 Ambassador Row in Longview and on the Internet at www.allseasonswindows.com.

Rader Funeral Home

Rader Funeral Home is a longstanding member of the Longview community and a leader in the funeral home industry. Its modern, fourteen-thousand-square-foot facility, the largest in Longview, is one of the finest and most modern funeral homes anywhere.

Its home-like atmosphere, tasteful artwork and warm, pleasing décor, combined with the best service anywhere, has made Rader Funeral Home the number one choice among Longview residents in their time of need.

The Rader family tradition of service now spans three generations. It dates back to the late 1920s when a young Illinois man named LeRoy Rader decided to become a mortician. After graduating from mortuary school in Chicago, LeRoy eventually moved to Paris, Texas, where he took a job with Emerson-Brown-Roden Funeral Home.

A few years later, LeRoy moved his family to Longview to work with Welch Funeral Home, which eventually led to a promotion as manager of the Everett and Welch Funeral Home in Gladewater.

In 1936, LeRoy Rader and Thomas Welch formed a partnership and opened the Welch and Rader Funeral Home in Kilgore. LeRoy soon purchased his partner's interest and changed the name to Rader Funeral Home, thus founding what would become an East Texas landmark.

In the early 1950s, LeRoy purchased a funeral home on North Fredonia Street adjacent to the First Methodist Church in Longview. He asked his son, Charley, who had just graduated from North Texas State University, to manage it. In 1954, Charley and his wife, Betty, moved to Longview, where they ran the funeral home and became active in the community.

In 1970 the family built its current facility at 1617 Judson Road, expanding its space and bringing a new level of comfort and service to the Longview community. Then, in 1981, Betty and Charley's son, Charles, returned to work with the family business after graduating from Texas Tech University and Dallas Institute of Funeral Services.

Another third-generation family member joined the business in 1985 when Betty and Charley's daughter, Lynn Martin, began handling public relations and advertising. In 1989 the family expanded its business by opening Rosewood Park Cemetery and Mausoleum in North Longview.

Rader Funeral Home has become a leader in the industry because of the Rader tradition of thoughtful, caring service that is a family tradition and an enduring Longview legacy.

❖

Above: The original Rader Funeral Home building on Fredonia Street in Longview, Texas.

Below: Rader Funeral Home's current location at 1617 Judson Road in Longview, Texas.

Gregg County Historical Commission

The perseverance of Gregg County's John Ben Sheppard (1915-1990) and others interested in Texas historical preservation paid off when the Texas Legislature in 1953 created the Texas Historical Survey Committee. The name was changed to the Texas Historical Commission in 1973. It was not until 1962 when Gregg County Judge R. E. "Peppy" Blount appointed the Gregg County Historical Survey Committee with Mrs. Paul (Amelia) Belding as chairman. Belding named Dr. Norman W. Black as vice-chairman. Black remained in this position except for the 1991-1992 term when E. R. McWhorter was vice-chairman. The Gregg County Historical Commission is an arm of the county government and its sixteen members are appointed in odd-numbered years, when the Texas Legislature meets, by the county judge and commissioners court. It is the responsibility of the historical commission to preserve Gregg County's historical heritage and to encourage others to do the same.

❖

Top: The Gregg County Courthouse, c. 1879.

Middle: The Gregg County Courthouse, c. 1897.

Bottom: The Gregg County Courthouse, c. 1932.

Some of the functions of the Gregg County Historical Commission are:

- Monitoring the county's 112 historical markers and sites for damages and other maintenance needs.
- Maintaining a list of books pertaining to Gregg County, Texas and local history written by local authors and serving as a repository for these books.
- Sponsoring Junior Historian and the Webb Society chapters at local schools and LeTourneau University.
- Providing assistance to the twenty-two heritage organizations within the county.
- Monitoring and supporting the county's museums: the Gregg County Historical Museum, the East Texas Oil Museum, the Kilgore Rangerette Showcase, the Gladewater Historical Museum, and the Longview Museum of Fine Arts.
- Providing support and assistance for archeological funds and to participate on site if needed.
- Monitoring the Gregg County Courthouse campus and historic pecan trees.
- Providing the Official Flag of Gregg County for county-owned buildings.
- Attending conferences pertaining to historical preservation.
- Assisting TxDOT and FHA with inspections.
- Cooperating with other county historical commissions, especially neighbors.

SPRING HILL STATE BANK

Organizers of Spring Hill State Bank had faith in the community at a time when others still had doubts. The seven men who came together to organize the bank recognized the potential of the Spring Hill area and applied for a bank charter in 1975.

But the Texas Department of Banking doubted there was enough business in the area to support a bank and rejected the initial charter application. That didn't stop Theo Ellison, Paul French, Chapple C. Dowell, Gene Clark, William Jerry Williams, Jim Heath and Billy Don Thomas.

They were all connected to the Spring Hill community in northern Gregg County and understood the potential there. The group worked with well-known attorney and former State Senator Jack Strong and two years later on September 19, 1977, Spring Hill State Bank opened for business.

Organizers set out to develop and maintain a sound financial institution that was clearly recognized by the public and the media as one that offers quality service to its chosen markets and produces a fair return to stockholders.

That philosophy proved its worth in the oil and real estate bust of the 1980s. High-priced oil led to over development of Texas' real estate market and the desire to capitalize on the growth led many financial institutions to make loans that turned out to be unwise.

Spring Hill State Bank survived the bust. It was one of the few banks in the Longview/Tyler markets to survive this period of financial collapse that has been described as Texas' worst economic period since the Great Depression.

The bank now has more than $100 million in total assets, employs 45 people at its main office at 3700 Gilmer Road and its branch office at 202 Hollybrook. The bank has over 8,000 deposit accounts and 3,400 loan accounts.

The bank continually supports community nonprofit activities such as United Way, the Longview Chamber of Commerce, LEDCO, Junior Achievement, Pilot Club, Rotary, Junior League, Kidsview and many other charitable organizations.

The bank's employees have taken a leadership role in many organizations. Its employees, managers and stockholders will continue to be involved in the local community. They also will work hard to make sure the bank remains an independent locally owned institution offering high-quality financial services to area residents for years to come.

For more information and office locations, Spring Hill State Bank is located on the Internet at www.springhillbank.com.

Richard Parker Plumbing

Top: Virginia, Richard, and their son Glenn, 1977.

Above: Richard and Virginia with their son Glenn, daughter Ginger and her son Spencer, 2004.

The Parker family has been providing high quality plumbing services in East Texas for over sixty years, and they plan to continue that tradition for generations to come. Today, Richard Parker Plumbing is known as the place to call for fair prices and first-rate workmanship, having been awarded the "Best of East Texas" Award in 1993, 1995, and 1997.

The Parkers' business ventures began in Pittsburg, Texas with William Jefferson Parker, who was the senior partner in the Parker-Bardwell blacksmith shop, and later tried his hand at running a country grocery store. In 1941, one of his sons, William "Bill" Parker, took a job with the city water department as a meter reader and repairman, traveling from house to house by bicycle. He later began to take a few small plumbing jobs for people he met through his job, and in 1945 he resigned from the water department to open his own plumbing business.

Two year later, Bill's brother Charles H. "Posey" Parker, a World War II veteran, joined the business. While their relationship remained congenial, after five years of working side-by-side the brothers decided to split the business into two separate shops.

Posey's two sons, Richard Lynn Parker and James Mikel Parker, were raised in the plumbing business. The youngest son, Mikel, stayed in Pittsburg and worked at his father's plumbing company, while the older son, Richard Lynn, moved to Longview along with his wife Virginia in 1974, and opened his own firm, Richard Parker Plumbing.

Richard Lynn and Virginia's son, Richard Glenn Parker, was born in 1975, and he started going on calls with his father as a toddler. Like his dad, he was raised in the plumbing business, and he began to work alongside his father as a teenager, joining the business full time in 1992.

A civic-minded family, many of the Parkers have been involved with their community. Richard Lynn has served on the Longview Plumbing Advisory Board, volunteered with the Red Cross, served as chaplain with the Gregg County Jail Ministry, worked with the Boy Scouts, and is a member of the Longview Lions Club.

Today, Richard Parker Plumbing offers home and commercial repair services, drain cleaning, and operates a retail parts store known for carrying hard to find plumbing parts. It is solely a family business, where father and son perform all the plumbing work, while wife and mother Virginia mans the store. The business has never operated more than four or five trucks at one time, and the Parkers have kept the firm small to ensure they can provide the highest quality service.

Another generation of Parkers has joined the business and Spencer Andrew Parker has been tagging along with his grandpa Richard Lynn, helping to carry tools since he could walk. At age seven, Spencer has become a local celebrity, starring in Richard Parker Plumbing television commercials and he plans to someday head up the family business.

STEMCO, LP

Specialized Truck Equipment Manufacturing Company, or STEMCO, is known throughout the world as the supplier of the highest quality wheel-end components to the heavy and medium-duty commercial vehicle markets.

The company began on March 1, 1951, when Ben Cook and Tom Davidson got together in St. Charles, Missouri, to make mufflers and oil reservoirs for trucks. In the summer of 1958, the company began a phased move to Longview.

As the market changed, STEMCO branched out into dual wheel adapters, hubo hose carriers, drum check gauges and exhaust accessories. An important development occurred in 1951 when Tom Arnold, the company's chief engineer, designed the STEMCO Hub Oil Seal and Hub Cap, which used oil rather than grease to lubricate wheel bearings.

At first, few believed oil could be retained in the hub. STEMCO's product eventually convinced mechanics and maintenance personnel, and the company extended applications to trucks and tractors two years after introducing it on trailers. A few years later, Arnold introduced the see-through window in the hubcap and the product line started to sell.

By 1961, STEMCO had persuaded some original equipment manufacturers to equip trucks with oil seals as standard components. Other important milestones included acquisition by Garlock, Inc., an industrial packing and sealing company (1964), the first Grit Guard seals for severe service (1968), pinion seals (1969) and oil seals for medium-duty trucks (1973). Following Garlock's acquisition by Colt Industries in 1975, STEMCO began marketing Monroe moisture ejectors.

By 1979 oil lubrication had captured ninety percent of the heavy truck and trailer market. Five years later, STEMCO acquired Engler Instruments in New Jersey, a company known for its line of accurate hubodometers. In 1996, STEMCO introduced the Sentinel Hub Cap, the first in the world to keep water completely out of the wheel end.

STEMCO's first fully electrometric lip seal, the Guardian HP, was introduced in 1997, extending seal life performance and providing an advanced technology wheel-end sealing solute to the commercial vehicle market.

The following year in 1998, STEMCO released the Voyager Seal, its first fully unitized, hub-installed seal. With advances in sealing, hubcap, and bearing retention and adjustment technology, STEMCO combined high-performance products into a comprehensive wheel-end package.

Over the next few years, additional part numbers and product lines were released. Throughout its history, STEMCO has nurtured a global reputation for quality products. It now serves Canada, Europe, Australia, Latin America, Japan, Southeast Asia, South Africa, and the Middle East.

Today, more than thirty percent of STEMCO sales are from new products introduced within the last five years. The company has several pending projects under development, and looks forward to continued new product introductions for years to come.

For more information about STEMCO, please visit www.stemco.com.

Homewood Suites by Hilton

You're never far from home when you stay at Longview's Homewood Suites by Hilton. Our upscale all-suite residential-style hotel is designed to make you feel at home when you are on the road for a few days or more.

Suites are designed to make guests feel like they are at home and offer amenities that other hotels just cannot match. The best part is we do it at a price that will make you wonder why you have been settling for less.

That is because our suites provide guests with the comfort, convenience and privacy of home for the price of a traditional hotel room. Amenities include spacious one-bedroom, two-bedroom and/or studio suites with fully equipped kitchens, daily complimentary hot breakfast and an evening Manager's Reception Monday through Thursday with a light meal and beverages.

Homewood Suites by Hilton is perfect for guests who travel on field assignments, relocate to a new community or attend seminars, conventions or corporate training programs. Leisure travelers on vacation also find our suites perfect for meeting their needs.

The Longview facility stands out among its peers as the recipient of the Longview Beautification Award. Our guests know they can expect an attractive atmosphere, peace and quiet, and all the comforts and convenience of home.

Our hotel features a unique "lodge" where business and leisure travelers relax and socialize. Amenities include an exercise center, swimming pool, outdoor sports court, and business center with computer, modem, printer, photocopier and access to a fax machine.

Complimentary maid service and complimentary grocery shopping service are provided. You will also find an on-site twenty-four hour "Suite Shop" convenience store, coin laundry, laundry/valet service, complimentary beverage area, safety deposit box, audio/visual equipment rental and meeting rooms.

Homewood Suites by Hilton features two types of suites—a regular suite, and a suite with an expanded living room. Each Homewood suite is equipped with a king-size bed or two double queen beds, a full-size fold-out sofa in the living room, ceiling fans, two remote-controlled color televisions, spacious and well-lit dining areas, iron and ironing board and a fully equipped kitchen with a microwave, full-size refrigerator with icemaker, coffeemaker, twin-burner stove, and kitchen utensils.

You will also receive our "Unconditional One Hundred Percent Satisfaction Guarantee." We'll make it right, or your night's stay is free. Come and see what makes Longview's Homewood Suites by Hilton your home away from home.

Gans & Smith Insurance Agency, Inc.

Gans & Smith Insurance Agency, Inc. is Longview's oldest insurance agency. Founded in 1889 by J. R. and T. E. Clemmons, Gans & Smith has operated continuously in Longview despite changes in East Texas and the insurance industry itself.

The agency assumed its present name in 1912 under the partnership of W. Bruner Smith and Daniel W. Gans. Present owners are Hermes E. Payne, Jr., David L. McWhorter, Philip G. Smith, Hank Smith and Mark T. Ramsey.

Although the partners have changed several times through the years, the name has remained the same, and so have the principles that have made the company a success. Gans & Smith is dedicated to providing proper insurance programs to clients through the coordinated efforts of its staff and the many insurance companies it represents.

The company is committed to providing competitive pricing without sacrificing or compromising the needs of its customers. Its employees, who number around thirty, service those needs in a timely and effective manner, maintaining a constant willingness to help.

The first Gans & Smith office was in the original First National Bank Building at 200 North Fredonia. It later moved to the Longview National Bank site at 213 Fredonia, and in 1972 moved to its current location at 1109 Judson Road. The agency has expanded to meet its growing needs and added a branch office at 4000 South Medford Drive in Lufkin.

The agency sells and services a wide range of insurance products for individuals and businesses. Those include property, liability, life and personal lines of insurance as well as bonds, workers compensation and employee benefits products.

The firm sells its products through nationally recognized, financially sound companies with reasonable and competitive rates. It works with a wide range of companies and keeps abreast of the latest insurance coverages in order to offer our customers the best coverage from the best company at the best price.

Gans & Smith believes in giving back to the community and the insurance industry. It is actively involved in Leadership Longview, Longview Rotary Club, Kiwanis Club and other civic organizations. David McWhorter and R.H. "Bobby" Smith both have served as Longview mayor, Les Pruett is past president of the Independent Insurance Agents of Texas and David McWhorter serves on its board of directors.

Although the firm takes pride in its civic and industry contributions, it is service to its customers that comes first because the firm never loses sight of the fact that it exists to meet its customers' insurance needs.

For more information about Gans & Smith Insurance, please visit www.gans-smith.com.

Dedicated to providing competitive pricing without compromising the true needs of our customers.

Noble Enterprises

Gene Noble has taken his business from a one-man security operation run out of his kitchen, to the leading provider of security services in East Texas with an office staff of twelve and a security force that tops off at ninety. In the past three years alone, Noble Enterprise's business has doubled and they now provide all types of private security services in twenty-six Texas counties as well as maintaining an office in Shreveport, Louisiana.

Noble Enterprises and Noble Security were born in February 1989, after Gene was approached by oil giant STEMCO to help them better secure a nearby industrial facility. Having recently lost a bid to become Gregg County Sheriff by just ten percent of the vote, Gene was at the time considering a job offer to direct a police academy in the Metroplex area. He reviewed STEMCO's situation and reported that an internal security department would solve their problems. But STEMCO wanted to outsource that security force, and knowing that Gene had years of law enforcement experience and expertise, they asked him to run it.

After much prayer and discussion with his wife, Gene decided to start his own security firm. He hired two employees, and set to work. The business quickly took off, adding new clients including the Made Rite Company and several area banks.

Before long Noble Security expanded its services and in August 1989 started providing pre-employment screening to help clients hire quality employees. In 1992 the firm began offering drug prevention and detection training and two years later they added a patrol service, which today employs eight officers who make their rounds in four patrol vehicles. In 1998 both residential and commercial alarm and CCTV system services were launched and the firm is now part of a nationwide network that offers the highest quality alarm and fire alarm products. The same year a fleet of three armored vehicles was added, making Noble the only private armored car service in Northeast Texas.

Today Noble offers a full range of security services including on-site security with uniformed, armed or unarmed officers; regular and late-night armored car services; armed patrol services; pre-employment screening and drug testing; random drug testing; CCTV installation and maintenance; remote video monitoring; private investigation services; and the installation, maintenance, and monitoring of burglar, fire, medical, and access control alarm systems. Gene is proud of the low turnover rate of his security officers, who are prescreened and then trained at the company's in-house academy. He hires the best, most reliable and professional personnel, who can, in turn, offer outstanding security services to his customers.

For more information about Noble Enterprises and Noble Security, please visit www.noblesecurity.com.

Good Shepherd Health System

In 2005, Good Shepherd Medical Center celebrated seventy years of innovation in healthcare services and dedication to the health and well being of East Texas residents. Through continuous community support, the once forty-seven bed Gregg Memorial Hospital has expanded to a 412-bed regional referral center offering highly-skilled care in a variety of specialties, including cardiology, emergency care, oncology, orthopaedics, neurology, surgery, and women's and pediatric services.

Many East Texas families have seen multiple generations born at Good Shepherd. In 2003, Good Shepherd introduced the only neonatal intensive care unit (NICU) between Dallas and Shreveport to care for infants born as early as twenty-eight weeks gestation and those with special needs.

The Health System has seven Family Health Centers located throughout the region to provide primary care. In 2005, Good Shepherd Health System acquired a twenty-five-bed critical access hospital in Linden.

Good Shepherd has earned national recognition for its quality services. For the past three years, the Medical Center received the Distinguished Hospital Award for Clinical Excellence™ from HealthGrades®, which places Good Shepherd among the top five percent of all acute-care hospitals in the country in terms of overall clinical excellence across a broad array of services.

Good Shepherd Health System is a not-for-profit organization, funded solely from patient revenue and community support through the Good Shepherd Foundation. The mission has always been to provide quality, compassionate and comprehensive healthcare services to every patient. Good Shepherd Medical Center is located at 700 East Marshall Avenue in Longview, Texas and on the Internet at www.GoodShepherdHealth.org.

❖

Above: Good Shepherd Medical Center is a 412-bed, not-for-profit, community-owned hospital dedicated to creating a healthier future for the residents of Longview and Northeast Texas.

Below: Medical Plaza is comprised of three medical office towers and houses Good Shepherd Ambulatory Surgical Center and seventy physicians representing sixteen different specialties.

Skeeter Performance

Holmes Thurmond designed the original bass fishing boat, Skeeter, in 1948. Dubbed "Skeeter" because its needle nose reminded people of a mosquito, these fast, narrow crafts made of molded marine plywood immediately caught the attention of area fishermen because of their stability and sleek design. Known from the start for its commitment to recreational anglers, today Skeeter prides itself on its reputation as a company that listens to its customers.

Initially manufactured in Marshall, Texas, Skeeter boats were sold through Reeves Marine in nearby Shreveport, Louisiana, which today is still a Skeeter dealer. As new materials became available in the 1950s, Skeeter was one of the first innovators to use fiberglass to construct its boats, making it possible to manufacture larger quantities of Skeeters in a variety of sizes and styles.

In 1961, STEMCO purchased the company and moved its plant to a larger facility in Longview, Texas. Several innovations were made in the following years, including the development of a series of hulls with names like the popular Super Skeeter, Sweet Thing, and Hawk.

The company's rapid growth necessitated another move, to its current plant in Kilgore, Texas in the early 1970s. In 1975 Skeeter developed the first v-bottom bass boat, which was equipped with a powerful 150 horsepower engine. These high-speed performance boats were the first of their kind and proved popular with anglers on the then-fledging bass fishing tournament circuits.

Hull innovation has always been a Skeeter trademark and when it unveiled the first Starfire 175 in 1979, its groundbreaking design and interior made it the world's premiere bass fishing boat.

In 1983 the Coleman Company purchased Skeeter and developed its first combination ski and fishing boat. With the increasing popularity of competitive bass fishing in the south, Skeeter also introduced its first SX model, which featured an amazing blend of speed, performance and style.

The 1990s saw the new ZX Series of bass boats, which incorporated advanced hull designs with modern styling. At this time, walleye tournament fishing was beginning to gain popularity north of the Mason-Dixon Line and Skeeter responded by producing a line of deep v-boats made especially for walleye anglers.

In the mid 1990s Skeeter brought a crew of aerospace engineers to its design team. Using the latest technology and software, these engineers helped develop one of the first composite boats available in the U.S., the ZX202.

Skeeter began factory packaging all of its boats with Yamaha outboard motors in 1996, following the firm's purchase by the Yamaha Boat Company. Teaming up with the world's most technologically advanced outboard engine manufacturer furthered Skeeter's quest to produce the ulitimate fishing boat.

The new millennium brought Jay Yelas, a Skeeter pro staff angler, the first ever triple crown winner of all three major bass fishing titles, along with two consecutive angler of year awards. A new line of saltwater boats was also introduced, upping the Skeeter line to twenty-five models of watercrafts.

From the tiny wooden boat crafted over fifty years ago, Skeeter's tradition of excellence has helped make it a leader in today's fishing boat industry.

BEST WESTERN INN OF KILGORE

A sweetheart of a hotel, the Best Western Inn of Kilgore first opened its doors on Valentine's Day 1997. Owned by Balram LLC, a proprietor of several local lodging establishments, the Best Western is located near downtown Kilgore on North Highway 259 near Interstate Highway 20.

The hotel features forty-three guest rooms, including two suites, and two Jacuzzi suites. Each room has a twenty-five inch television with cable and HBO, an iron and ironing board, micro-refrigerator, coffeemaker, hair dryer, data port, AM/FM clock radio, air conditioning, and high-speed Internet service. Non-smoking and handicapped accessible rooms are also available. Guests are offered free local calls, the use of an outdoor pool, and a complimentary continental breakfast featuring fresh Belgian waffles.

Business travelers enjoy the hotel's fax and photocopying services, as well as the proximity to Kilgore College and several area corporations including Vertex and Halliburton. All guests are treated to clean, spacious rooms, free parking, twenty-four hour front desk service, and ice and vending machines. Several restaurants are within walking distance of the property, as well as a brand new Wal-Mart Supercenter. The facility is part of the Best Western chain, which is a membership association of independently owned and operated hotels offering more than three hundred thousand quality guest rooms. Founded in 1946 the chain began as an informal link between lodging establishments and today operates over four thousand properties in eighty-three countries, making it the largest hotel brand in the world.

The Best Western Inn of Kilgore is located on the site of the old Streamliner restaurant, a once-popular eatery that featured a railroad car as a dining room. When the land was cleared for construction, the railroad car was donated to the City of Kilgore.

The hotel was planned and built by Naresh "Nick" Patel, a former landscaper turned contractor, whose family has been in the hospitality business for many years. Patel worked tirelessly to complete the hotel and other properties and was gaining great success in the industry until his untimely death. Today, The Best Western Inn of Kilgore is run by Naresh's widow Kersti and fellow Balram partners, along with the help of assistant manager Teresa Clayton. Sons Janti, Nikesh, and Frank hope to someday continue their father's legacy and join the family business.

U.S. TITLE COMPANY, INC.

Stephen McDaniel and U.S. Title Company, Inc., have provided Gregg County with over twenty-two years of computerized title searches and title insurance. Opening in March 1984 in Longview's historic Whaley House as the first computerized title plant in Gregg County, U.S. Title has grown to serve Harrison, Sabine, and Upshur Counties in East Texas. In 1986, U.S. Title relocated to its present location at 1000 North High Street in Longview, Texas.

A graduate of Baylor University Law School in 1969, McDaniel came to Longview in 1973 to join the law firm of Sharp, Ward and Ross, after serving four years as a Special Agent with the Federal Bureau of Investigation. Wanting to make a change in property title law and record keeping, which had not changed in more than a century, McDaniel ventured into building his own database for Gregg County. In July 1983, with forty employees working two shifts of twenty, it took almost a year to put more than a century's worth of deeds, titles, and transactions on the database. The database is constantly updated and currently includes several million entries in just Gregg County.

According to McDaniel, "Computerization is now the norm for the industry, but placing such an emphasis on computers in the early 1980's was much more expensive than today and building a database was also very tedious work. In the end, our clients benefitted from the quick and accurate records. Unfortunately, 1984 was a time of great drops in the price of oil and one of the worst economic environments for banking and real estate in fifty years. It was a tough, tough time, but with the help of many good friends, loyal customers and God's blessings, we survived the '80s and that was no small accomplishment."

While pre-packaged title software programs were available, McDaniel felt there was a better way. With the help of a Longview computer expert, Leonard Knipe, a program was written specifically for U.S. Title.

After word spread of the success and ease of access at U.S. Title's plant, there were requests from others across the state to use the same software system. At this point, Southwest Database, Inc., was formed to build title plants for others in Texas.

Hamp Smead, a Longview attorney, joined McDaniel to expand the business, and in February 1987, opened a data entry company on the island of Barbados, changing the name from Southwest Database, Inc. to International Data Services, Ltd. The new operation opened at the Hadley House, St. George Street in Bridgetown, Barbados, West Indies. Longtime employees Renae Tennimon and Debbie Thompson were two of the very first data entry employees in Longview.

According to Stephen and his wife, Marcia, their children, Steve and Erin, gave the impetus to develop attachments to many community efforts. From supporting Junior League community projects, to serving as deacon and Sunday school teacher at the First Baptist Church, to serving on the Trinity School of Texas Board of Directors, Stephen points out that it has all been a privilege.

❖

Above: Stephen and Marcia McDaniel with their daughter, Erin. Stephen has served as president of the Longview Museum of Fine Arts Board of Directors, chairman of the East Texas Regional Airport Economic Development Board, as well as a board member for the Cherokee Club and Neal McCoy's Angel Network. Marcia is a registered interior designer with the Architectural Board of Texas, doing business as J&S Design in Longview.

Top, right: (From left to right) Hamp Smead, Stephen McDaniel, and Leonard Knipe.

Right: Stephen and Marcia McDaniel.

2C Processor USA, LLC Texas

Don and Charlotte Esch, both successful East Texas entrepreneurs, began marketing in January 2001 to provide merchants and businesses with totally automated payment solutions. Charlotte assists in the business and also operates a state-of-the-art piano studio with digital pianos and computerized programs for optimum learning.

Don is considered an expert in the industry and is one of three regional offices of 2C Processor USA, LLC, a national Los Angeles-based company that is registered MSP/ISO in association with Bank of America and Chase Merchant Services, LLC. In addition, processing alliances have been formed with Cynergy Data, and Global E Telecom. The Texas regional office of 2C Processor USA provides credit card, debit, and ATM card processing, electronic check guarantee, gift and loyalty cards, wireless credit card processing, payroll debit card, NSF check recovery and equipment sales and leasing. It regularly analyzes merchant processing statements as a free service and recommends high-technology solutions for more efficient processing. In most cases, merchants can enjoy an instant rate reduction simply by allowing 2CPUSA to reprogram their existing machines.

The 2CPUSA Texas regional office has successfully established high-technology processing for the automotive dealership industry, healthcare arena, industrial electronics, liquor store and grocery/convenience store markets, processing approximately $1 million monthly for local and interstate commerce. 2CPUSA also serves smaller merchants, and strives to educate all businesses of the most economic processing solutions available, as technology progresses. For more information, please call 903-291-0888 or visit www.clickonyes.com.

Texas Regional Manager Don Esch.

J. A. Kay Roofing

In the late 1960s, John Kay literally learned roofing from the ground up…by carrying shingles up ladders. In 1974 Kay launched his own business venture when he founded Kay's Roofing in the Gilmer/Daingerfield area.

Two years later, Kay partnered with father-in-law Ben McWhorter, to establish Kay-Mac Roofing. The business eventually settled, after several location changes, on Standard Street in the Greggton area.

In 1984, Kay again set out on his own and re-established Kay's Roofing, which is today known as J. A. Kay Roofing, a licensed contractor with the City of Longview. Providing high quality workmanship is the company's hallmark and Kay is proud of the many Better Business Bureau Gold Star awards he has received in recognition of the firm's outstanding record of no customer complaints.

Kay has carefully limited his company's growth to ensure his employees, who include his two sons and his brother-in-law, install the best roofs possible. In order to provide customers with quality materials, J. A. Kay Roofing is also a certified installer for GAF Material Corporation. For more information about J. A. Kay Roofing, contact them at 903-759-6745.

ROOFING

KAY-MAC ROOFING—Built-up roofs, re-roofing or nail-overs. Commercial-residential. 30 years experience. Free estimates, 759-4242.

Above: This advertisement appeared in the Longview Morning Journal *on July 19, 1981.*

Right: John and Benita Kay.

COURTESY OF SOUTHWEST STUDIOS.

About the Author

Van Craddock, Jr.

Van Craddock Jr., who calls himself an "amateur East Texas historian," has written a history-and-humor column for the *Longview News-Journal* since 1978. The Gladewater native is a graduate of Longview High School and Stephen F. Austin State University, where he majored in journalism and commercial art. He and wife Bettye, a journalism instructor at Kilgore College, have two grown children: Chris, a journalism teacher; and Cathy, an English teacher married to Matt Tenner. The Craddocks are members of Longview's First United Methodist Church.

Craddock served in Vietnam in the U.S. Army in 1971-72 and has published a book of his *News-Journal* columns titled, "I Would've Been a Lumberjack But I Couldn't Hack It." He's also a proud member of the Mayberry Union High Chapter of the Andy Griffith Show Rerun Watchers Club.